WANDJUK
M A R I K A

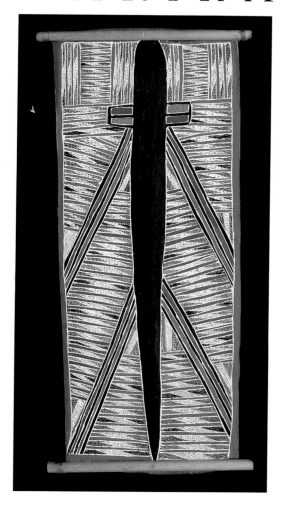

WANDJUK MARIKA

Life Story

As told to Jennifer Isaacs

UNIVERSITY OF QUEENSLAND PRESS

Wandjuk Marika Life Story

The Literature Centres in Yolŋu communities have developed their own phonetic script which reproduces the languages of north-east Arnhem Land more accurately than can be achieved with the English alphabet. This is the first book to utilise this typography for general readership.

The principal symbols and their pronunciation are:
ŋ = pronounced ng, as in sung
ä = long a, as in father
l, d, t = retroflex consonants formed with the tongue curled backwards against the palate.

Page 1: *Bark painting by Wandjuk Marika, 1982.*

Mawalan – the sacred walking stick of the Creation Ancestors.

Page 2: *Wandjuk Marika stands at the sacred Djaŋkawu place, Yalaŋbara, touched by the first rays of Walu, the sun.*

Running heads: *Detail of acrylic painting on canvas by Jimmy Barmula Yunupiŋgu, 1994.*

Yalaŋbara Sand Dunes.

Printed in Hong Kong by
South China Printing Co. Ltd.
Typeset by Character Typesetting Pty Ltd.

First published 1995 by
University of Queensland Press
Box 42, St Lucia, Queensland 4067
Australia

© text and paintings 1995 Wandjuk Marika's children: Janet Djanumbi, Alison Rärriwuy, Lynette Wayalwaŋa, Bruno Wuyula, Bruce Mawalan, Beth Giyakminy, Johnny Djaybiny, Pixie Napandala, Alfred Yalarrma, Nelson Gomili, Mary Jane Mayatili, Bruce Yalumul, Celina Bayulma, Lucille Dhawunyilinyil.

© editorial arrangement and notes 1995 Jennifer Isaacs.

Produced for the University of Queensland Press by Chapter & Verse, 1 King George Street, McMahons Point, NSW 2060.

Consulting poet: Rodney Hall.
Designed by John Witzig.
Edited by Carol Dettmann.

Cataloguing-in-Publication data
National Library of Australia

Marika, Wandjuk.
    Wandjuk Marika: life story
    ISBN 0 7022 2564 9

1. Marika, Wandjuk. 2. Aborigines, Australian – Biography. 3. Musicians – Australia – Biography. 4. Aboriginal Australian artists – Biography. 5. Aborigines, Australian – Land tenure – History. 6. Bark painting – Australia. 7. Aborigines, Australian – History. 8. Aborigines, Australian – Politics and government. I. Isaacs, Jennifer. II. Title
994.0049915

FOREWORD

Hello, my name is Mawalan Marika and I'm son of Wandjuk Marika, my father. This book is about my father's life story: he wanted to do this book to show his family, sons and daughters, and his great-granddaughters and their children for the future.

And I'm thinking about this book, it is really the good book for our future. Jenny Isaacs which I call her Ŋändi, that's my mother, she's been adopted to our family, she has been my family for a long time. She's in close touch with my family and she was the first woman who went to Yirrkala back in '69 I think, and met my father and my mother and became friends, and my mother adopted her and they become sisters. She [Jenny Isaacs] is also a Warramiri, the name of her tribe, and her skin name is Wurrapa she's also my mother 'cause she always look after me, when I get in touch with her she is always there. She was helping my father about 15 years and she got real family, David her husband, call my father wäwa (brother) and they have three boys: Yalaŋbara (Joe), Gurunda (Sam) and Lindirritj (Willy) — they are my wäwas, I call them brothers, my kid brothers. Whenever she goes to Yirrkala and she stay with us, we go out into the bush, I look after her; and we come to Sydney she always looks after me, she's my mother. Doesn't care that she is white but it's like my mother, they both the same and that's why she's helping me to do this book of my father's life story. And she's my real mother in this modern world like in Sydney.

Then I got another mother down at Melbourne too and I got sister there at Melbourne. Her name is Mayatili or her first name is Mary Jane and we've got the same blood, me and my sister. Because she's from Marika. Her mother is white but our blood is same and so I love all my family like brothers and sisters.

I have waited a long time for this book, I was wishing to hear how my father was doing that book. He wanted to do this book for himself and then he passed away in 1987. My father was working on it with my Ŋändi for long years, my mother Ŋändi — Jenny Isaacs — was helping. Now my father has passed away, I'm doing the same. He wanted to do this book by himself but he's gone — and that's why this book is.

Now we have made it and now we are going to publish his story.

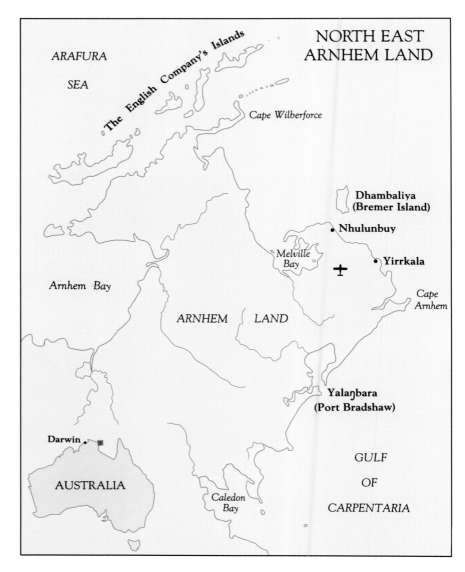

Not only the Aboriginals but for all people, all people throughout the world will recognise this book of my father's life story. I'm really looking forward to this book. It has been really hard for my Ŋä<u>nd</u>i, Jenny, but it will come out soon.

My family said don't publish this book for maybe eight years, but soon it will be time. It's our law not to mention the name of the person or man who's passed away. Now the family gave permission and at last it will be coming out next year. This book will be going out north, east, south and west.

And I hope you will love this book of my father's life story what he was doing back in those days when he was young. Thank you.

Mawalan Marika
Sydney 1994

Wandjuk and his grandson Djopani.

CONTENTS

Contents

PREFACE

Amongst indigenous people of the world, Wandjuk Marika was one of the great statesmen. His life's work has been compared to the front-line efforts by Black Elk and Chief Seattle to save native land and sovereignty in North America. As religious leader of the Rirratjiŋu people, he was also their teacher, master of ceremonial life and keeper of ritual and sacred truths.

Wandjuk Marika fought for justice for his own people in Australia – the Rirratjiŋu, and the communities of north-east Arnhem Land who collectively call themselves Yolŋu. Yolŋu lived a religious traditional lifestyle, caring for land and nature, and untroubled by modern industrial European values until the 1930s. Then came the impact of the Second World War, missionaries and anthropologists, drawing this area of Australia to national attention. When the beautiful red soil revealed its rich potential as bauxite, the Yolŋu were forced to launch the first legal battle for Land Rights against the mining giant Nabalco. Wandjuk Marika played a central role throughout this time, first as a young man (interpreting for his father Mawalan to anthropologists and making the first translation of the Bible into an Aboriginal language) and later assisting in the Land Rights case.

As Chairman of the Aboriginal Arts Board he introduced recognition of Aboriginal copyright and travelled throughout the world as cultural ambassador, artist and musician.

This book is Wandjuk's own story, told to me over several years (1984–87). After I worked with him during the Land Rights case and on many international projects related to traditional culture, Wandjuk asked me to help him make a book. He had seen many books appear from the stories and information he, his father and others had given researchers and anthropologists over 40 years, but none bore his name.

Wandjuk died suddenly in 1987. In keeping with Yolŋu protocol, his life story had to wait until his family gave permission for its release. Now, his concern and care for his children and his love and compassion for all people can at last be heard.

His children, particularly Mawalan and Rärriwuy, have worked hard with me to bring this book to completion so that his life and words can be heeded – a guiding message from the spirit world.

Jennifer Isaacs
Sydney 1995

Opposite: *Yothu Yindi, children of Djaŋkawu lands. Playing on the rocks at Yalaŋbara are Wandjuk's son and grandsons. Top: Djawulma. Middle from left: Birralimi, Yuwatjpi, Gulunŋura, Djopani. Bottom: Yalumul (son).*

NOTES

Wandjuk spoke this book, his life story, with a sense of urgency. He wanted to tell his children about his life and share his experience of the two worlds, Balanda and Yolŋu, so they would value their culture and the meaning of the land.

His story is also addressed to the wider Aboriginal family around the country, the people with whom he had "come together, know one another". In all these places he found one *story*, "the same *story*". This refers to the kinship between people traced from animals, plants and natural features of the landscape.

He begins his introduction selecting three

of his names – Wandjuk Djuwakan Marika. To Balanda, he was most often Wandjuk or Mr Marika. To his family he was Djuwakan which was also his grandfather's name. When he speaks of having "maybe 100 names", many of these are specific religious titles as he was grand master of ceremonies. He includes all the terms others used to refer to him – in Yolŋu life, the kinship name used also indicates the relationship of the speaker, so there are very many possibilities.

Throughout the book Wandjuk uses the term Yolŋu to mean Aborigines and the term Balanda to mean Europeans or non-Aboriginal people. All Aborigines of north-

east Arnhem Land use the word Yolŋu to denote themselves – literally "we the people". Yolŋu are divided into two groups of clans (Dhuwa and Yirritja), in anthropological terms "moieties". Wandjuk himself uses the term moiety due to his early work with anthropologists.

The word Balanda was also used by Yolŋu to refer to outsiders. "Balanda" is a derivative of the Dutch word "Hollander", introduced along with many other words, by the Macassans.

WHO I AM

In case you haven't seen me or know me, who I am, my name is Wandjuk Marika. I have more names, maybe I have 200 names or 100 names...yes 100, but I only use my two names – Wandjuk and Djuwakan, also Marika. Wandjuk Djuwakan Marika. This is the story I'm writing – so you can know **who** I am.

I am the full blood Aboriginal from top end of Australia, and I'm writing and I'm speaking from my own language but at the same time I'm translate to English – from my heart and from my mind – what I know about my life story. I am Aboriginal man, full blood Aboriginal, and I am talking and writing my own story, what I have been learn from my father until he was passed away. I been do it my own way to work. Not just from my own mind, but what my father taught me. I'm keeping myself on same track and line which is the one my father have been teaching me, so you can know who I am.

> When I am writing this book
> I can surely remember I am not like Balanda.
> I feel sad, I feel sad.
> When I tell you a story, I am **there** walking,
> I am **there** walking with my mother and father
> and I feel sad to look back and see
> what's been happening in my life.
> Sometime in the future my children will try to carry on
>   for me,
> the ceremonies, and caring for the land.

This is the story about my life, how I learn the two ways, Balanda and Yolŋu.
> When I was a little boy I did not know much about the
>   Balanda world.
> I thought: just the Yolŋu in the world, in Australia,
> nothing any Balanda, or white civilisation, nothing;
> because no one ever been able to tell me even in the school.

Opposite: *Dawn at the sacred landing site of Djaŋkawu at Yalaŋbara.*

Even when I went to school they did not tell me
what the Balandas were like,
or what the white
civilised life was like.
I don't know anything about it as a little boy;
just walk around learn about the Yolŋu culture,
learn about the Yolŋu life,
where to go,
how to find,
how to hunt and which is the certain places.
Which is my own land, where is the different moiety,
the different tribe which have the land
where that land *is*.

All those things I have done, I learned from my father and from different clans. In those days I don't know anything about the Balanda, nothing.

Then the Balanda recognise me that I am the man to handle all this culture and stand for the culture, traditional law – how to operate, how to teach the young people. Because I was learning this from my fathers, and mother taught me also.

Now I'm by myself.

I am talking about my life story, who I am and what I know, because there have been so many books written from my words, but it's all muddled up. I want to write in this book about my own life story, my experience and my knowledge – how *far* I know, what I have learned from my father, what my father learnt from his father's father's father's father. Now I know more simply and deeply, so I've written this book to show to my children and the Yolŋu, and also the Balanda, so they can know more about the Yolŋu life, Aboriginal life. There's many books that been written by the anthropologists, but it's been all muddle-up, doesn't make any sense. Sometimes they make me wild when I read their words. Their books make me very wild at it because they don't know much about nature, what's *in* the nature.

They don't know about the tree, **who** is the tree,
what the tree *is*.
They don't know **what** the grass *is*,
who is the grass or **what** is in the earth
and what *in* the mountain,
what *in* the trees.

Tree is tree, yes,
but we have individual names.
What is my tree and what is my mother's?
Which river is my grandmother or which mountain is also
     my mother … and my grandmother?

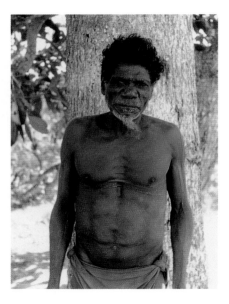

Wandjuk's father Mawalan Marika, clan leader of the Rirratjiŋu, 1959.

Opposite: *Wandjuk Marika – 1947 portrait taken by the anthropologist R.M. Berndt.*

14

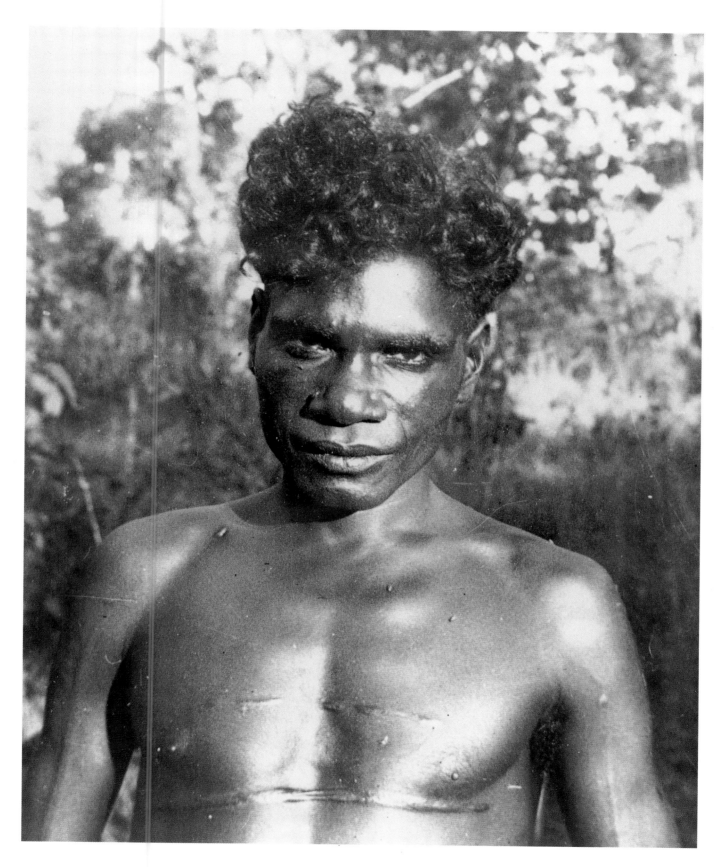

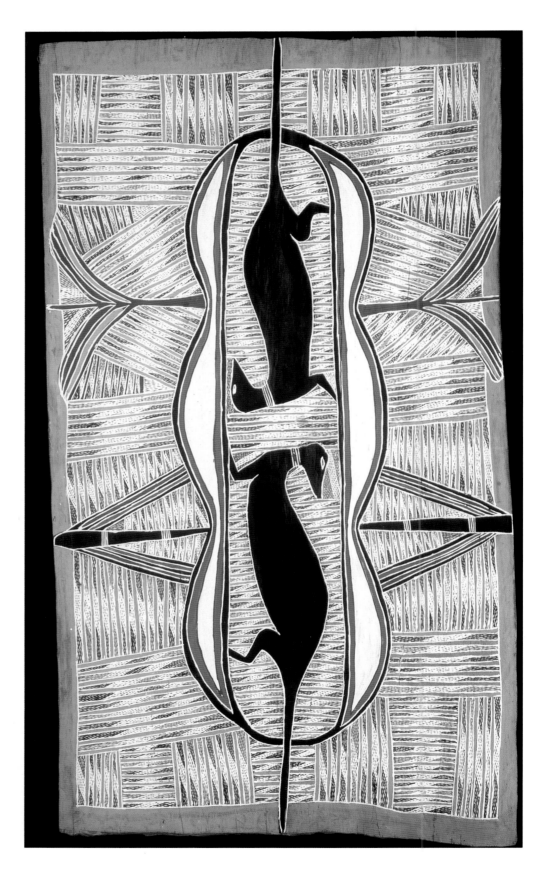

Bark painting by Wandjuk Marika, c. 1967.

As the Djaŋkawu walked along the sand dunes they saw the two Djanda (goannas). The sandhill shown surrounding the goannas is very sacred and is recreated at ceremonies as a mound of earth. The background design is the sand running down as the goannas walked up the dunes. The Djaŋkawu planted sacred djuta sticks in the ground with their feathered strings attached: these grew into trees.

Which food is a close relative to us Yolŋu.
We know which is which,
who owns the land
and how **far**.

Land is land, but there are different parts. Aboriginal people are different peoples, they have the names, the totems and the land owners. Yes, from beginning to end, every different tribe have a different knowledge and there is the story about how we become involved with each other, become relatives – by **totem**.

If I am travelling a different part of Australia I used to sit with Aboriginal people and learn and hear the story. Exactly the same story as from eastern Arnhem Land right up to Western Australia, wherever I have been travelling I sit with them and we talk each other what their relative or what their totem, what their symbol – and they always told exactly the same story as I have. They have different names, but their story is the same. We can call each other brothers and sisters, mothers and fathers through the creation, or totem, or sacred matters. All over Australia Aboriginal people are trying to be face to face, see each other, and walk together, share the knowledge, share the culture so **you** can know our culture that **you** don't know.

Our culture is so deeper and wise you don't know what's in it,
like tree have a name,
grass have a name,
and rock have a name,
bird have a name –
every different sort of bird or animals, flying things or
    crawling animal
or in the sea;
all names.
If we don't learn, one day it will be no more.
Some Balanda fully love the Aboriginal people
and visit to their Aboriginal community,
and when they leave, go back home
everybody's crying, sad,
because they like to be in Aboriginal community,
because they fall in love with their heart
to see and work and learn more about the Aboriginal way
    of life.

I want you to know this and think back how the Aboriginal people and European, or, in other words, black and white of Australia came to know each other. Can we work together, hand by hand, side by side, more than what we are now? In work together, not only just like we are now, but know each other, hand to hand, side by side. We had enough learning about the **English**, about the schooling. How about the Balanda for a change, to come and learn more about the Yolŋu culture or **Yolŋu** life?

I'm saying these words because I won't be here any longer,
but my word and my book will be the same for ever.
My word will be written.

I'm not only **talking** what I know, but I'm **translate** about my own story. Yolŋu know more English. I translate from our own language to English, so everyone can hear or read or know my own story, my own life. I didn't say [this] in my own language. I was translate from my own mind to English, so everyone can read my book and know who I am and what I am doing. Yes, in past I used to teach all the children. Then later I had been working for the whole world **and** teaching the children and show them the experience for their future. I give them experience so they can do as I did. The Yolŋu children might be able to go out into the world and meet the Balanda world; or they can carry on their work to teach their children and their children's children, in the Yolŋu world.

When my time is coming, they can know about
    my footsteps,
about my experience as I learnt from their grandfather
and I now just do the same,
show to my children.
Yes, not only that.
I'm not just talking from just the talk,
I'm talking from my heart,
deep from my heart to the young people today,
because I want to bring back the young people,
so they can carry on the knowledge, experience and power
for they belong too,
doesn't matter what part of Australia we live,
so west is north –
so we can come together, know each other,
work together, share the knowledge, share the experience.
That's what I want to see and this is what I'm writing
    to you,
to show the people.
There are many books that are written
but this is my own life story.

Shelter at Gäluru beach, near Nhulunbuy.

Now this is my own time, this is my own time. I'm moving out to my own area, Yalaŋbara Yirrkala is my spirit landing and also in that island Dhambaliya is my birth land, the land I was born in. Nhulunbuy is my spirit landing – where my father and my mother find me – and also today it is the township, the mining company township. Yirrkala is now run by the Yolŋu community. In the past it was run by the Methodist missionaries. Now I'm moving out, no one will tell me what to do or where to go.

I made up my mind,
I had enough trouble right round the world.
I have to do something to settle down
and work with my family

to show them what's in my mind.
I'm moving back to Yalaŋbara,
staying there now,
making my own family to settle down
and know more,
know about where to find the water
which I learnt when I was a little boy.
Now I settle down.
Today I'm on my way without no one to help,
but I do my best, standing with my own feet
to do what I want to do instead of just listening
to somebody else, somebody, someone,
listening to someone telling me what to do.
Now, I'm standing with my own feet
teaching my own children to stand,
carry the law.

*Wandjuk Marika's family camped at
Yalaŋbara, 1983.*

NOTES

Yalaŋbara, or sunrise beach, is the first and primary sacred area for all the Dhuwa peoples of eastern Arnhem Land, for when their main Creation Ancestors (the Djaŋkawu) were following the rays of the sun and the wulma cloud, they first came ashore here and then travelled across the country. The Djaŋkawu created all the people who are descended from them today and many special Djaŋkawu sites (waterholes, trees and wells) extend to central Arnhem Land.

The Djaŋkawu remain at Yalaŋbara as three large rocks, their canoe is visible in the shallows and other sacred places are still the physical manifestation of their presence. Wandjuk was the custodian of Yalaŋbara, a duty he felt to be the most important aspect of his being.

Above: *The spreading rays of the rising sun touched the waters of the sea, guiding the Creation Ancestors to the shore at Yalaŋbara.*

YALAŊBARA
MY BEAUTIFUL BEACH,
MY SACRED PLACE

When I was a little boy round about five years old, my father used to show me the land of Yalaŋbara, and teach me, show me, where to find the water, because this is very difficult for any Yolŋu or Balanda, for they don't know where to dig the hole to find the water, but I was five years old, and my father he told me.

He showed me the place where I have to dig for water,
because it is right on the sea,
the sea come and cover it up,
going out again,
and coming in,
that water is very special
and very sacred which is Djaŋkawu, Djaŋkawu created
    that water.
That fresh water is right on the beach
and mix with the salt water.
He taught me and showed me how to look after the place,
tell me to protect the land,
look after the land,
the Djaŋkawu story
and he showed me where He[1] is landed
where He is going
where is the sacred place,
and where is the place where they lived,
where they created
and that's when I was a little boy.

Then after that he teaching me how to fish and where to go, as [while] my mother was cooking the things they collected from the bush. They took [me] into the bush.

He used to told me the story,
the special ceremony,

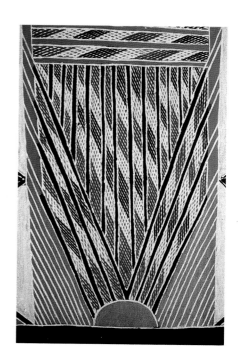

Painting by Wandjuk Marika's eldest son, Mawalan Marika.

Detail of Yalaŋbara sunrise design.

---
[1] Djaŋkawu.

Wandjuk Marika and Yalumul drinking fresh water from beneath the sand at Yalaŋbara.

to make me sleep every night.
Then I learn the story.
He also was singing, singing about the rhythm,
singing about the creation,
the public ceremony,
special song and special ceremony
every night.
Then I learnt through that about the song – while I
    was asleep.
He and my mother taught me.
My mother used to tell me about her totem,
her creation,
where she came from and her mother's.
This was the last thing they taught me before they
    passed away.
So, when I was grow up,
I know everything,
where to get food, how far to go, what kind of food.

Yalaŋbara is right on the beach, the coast, the east, there's the sand and sandhills. They taught me where to find the water we drink today on the beach. They taught me in the bush, show me things that **they** learnt when they were young. I learn exactly the same thing when I was a little boy. When I was a boy, my father was teach me many things, the story and the place, where the place belong to us for the Rirratjiŋu, how far the land which **is** our father and his father and his grandfather – where they have been **on** many, many years back. The land they passed on generation to generation until my father's time and he pass on to me when I was a little boy, and many are the stories I could tell you – *already there in the land.*

Now I began to grow up as a man.
This is the story of when I first come to Yalaŋbara
and he showed me and he said,
"This is the place.
Waŋarr maḏayin land (sacred ancestral land)
This is the place for us, maḏayin sacred place."
He said, "Look after this when I am gone."
Now I am looking after the sacred things and the sacred land
and many more.
They (my parents) taught me about the animal's names,
land creature and sea creature,
which is my mother's totem, I learnt from my mother,
that which is my own totem I learnt from father.
They used to taught me and showed me the place;
the Yirritja land, the Dhuwa land, yothu yindi (large, small)
    close together.
This is very close together, all one land.

*Wandjuk Marika collecting oysters
at Bawaka.*

And they have names, Yirritja and Dhuwa,
divided into two moieties like Rirratjiŋu and Gumatj.

And then when I was a boy I start to make the spear,
start to dig the hole for water,
where to find, started to hunt,
go to get,
how to make the spear good spear, or hand spear,
shovel nose spear, woomerah and stone spear,
guyarra which is stone spear's name.
Woomerah is galpu
and shovel nose spear is gayit,
all those things.

Who own that land, which is Yalaŋbara, sunrise.
Also who own the land which is sunset.
These are owned by Rirratjiŋu, two groups.
Sunset beach is owned by Roy and his family.
The sunrise is owned by Mawalan and his father, Djuwakan,
and now, today, I am the owner of that land,
Yalaŋbara or sunrise, and also Wukaka and all his family
and my family, we own that sunrise, Yalaŋbara.

Djaybiny, Wandjuk's son, digs beneath the white sands of Yalaŋbara to find the fresh water created by the Djaŋkawu.

There are so many waters on the beach.
When you walking along the beach you think there's
    nothing in it,
no water, just the sea,
of course it *is* sea, but under the beach or sand there is
    the water.
You could dig that sand and there is the fresh water,
but the salt water is on top and the fresh water is under
    the ground,
and then if you go to Guluruŋa, sunset – exactly the same
all the water is under the ground on the beach,
and the sea is on top of the earth,
and you see when you go along there for fishing –
you hardly ever see any water, but there *is* water,
doesn't matter about high tide, beneath the ground you find
    fresh water,
low tide, the same –
that sort of thing I learn when I was a little boy,
and then when I am seven years old he took me across
    the bush
across the land Dhalingbuy or Arnhem Bay
which is Wangurri tribe's land and outstation for the group
and the airstrip today.
Before, nothing was there when my father took me,
only people who live there in bush and they make
    us ceremony
to make me a young man and they teach me more about
    the law.

When I become a young man he taught me two culture, or three, or four, like Wangurri, Däṯiwuy, Dhalwaŋu which is my father's mother, then also Ŋaymil, Marrakulu, Marraŋu, and then many more – Gumatj and my own, Rirratjiŋu. Then when I was about eight he taught me about ceremony and song. We used to have a big tree with ŋatha (food), dhaŋgi[2] sour grass, and the palm tree gulwirri with the palm nut which is very dangerous and poison. My mother used to collect that food for everybody and they get nuts out of the shell, put them into the sun for five days or two or three days until they are very hard and dry, then hit with rocks and pounded them and put into dilly bag and take them to the water and soak for seven days. Then all the poison gone in the water. They pick up and if the smell of it, it's not fresh, it's ready to make bread. And, while they were doing that ceremony was been on for me, to make me the young man and my family has a feast or party with that food, because my father and mother happy that I am not young man any more, that I am initiated, circumcision, make me a man. My father and mother was happy, that I am

---

2   pound up the grass for fish poison (like lemon grass)

Yalaŋbara sand dunes, a most sacred area where the Djaŋkawu performed their creative acts and gave birth to the people.

The old airstrip at Port Bradshaw. Yalaŋbara (sunrise) beach is along the top right; Guluruŋa (sunset) beach is at the top left. The land in the foreground belongs to Gumatj Yirritja people.

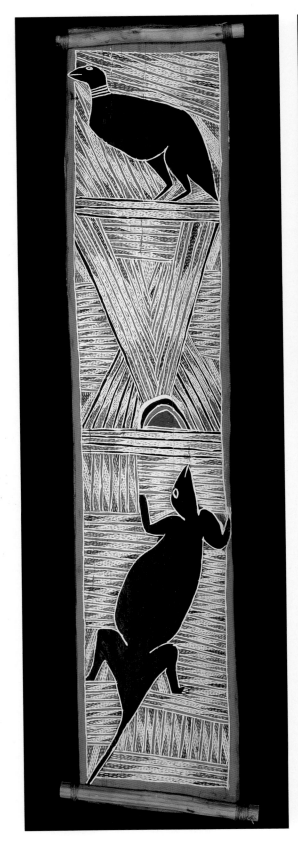

their son, their first son, before my sisters, and that why now I know more about their culture, more about their story.

> Yes, this is a long time ago,
> which I recall about my forefathers,
> my father's father's father's father, after the Djaŋkawu
>   arrived
> he is the name of that sunrise – Miliḏitjpi.
> Yes, Miliḏitjpi is the name of the sunrise,
> Yalaŋbara.
> After Miliḏitjpi, there is my father's grandfather
> and his son is Djuwakan,
> and after Djuwakan, my father Mawalan
> and he is the sunrise, also.

> And after that Djaŋkawu divided into two groups,
> one group for sunrise and one group for sunset.
> But we are still the same people, we are still the same,
> the same religion, group.

Sunset is Roy's family and his brother's family, and on my side, on the sunrise, is Wukaka, myself, Mayakaŋu, Mawalan the second, all my family and all of my sons. Roy's father's name, which is my young brother's name. (Don't call him – too early for me to call his name, he's passed away.[3]) He own the sunset, Guluruŋa sunset.

Before my father passed away, he tell me, teach me how to look after, protect the land, not only Yalaŋbara sunrise, but whole of the areas right up to Seven Mile Beach, and also I could teach the sunrise people what the sacred object. You can hear about us, we used to be called bottom Rirratjiŋu and top Rirratjiŋu, at Yirrkala, that's the sunrise and sunset. There is also bottom Djapu and top Djapu, then there is many more also Gumatj, Djambarrpuyŋu (Bremer Island), and top Djambarrpuyŋu (Arnhem Bay), same design, same maḏayin. But they own and talk same languages, well this is the same.

> It start from Djaŋkawu.
> He divided up two people, two Rirratjiŋu,
> and another thing,
> we are one clan, one language, one song and one
>   everything,
> but He put it on two sides.
> When the ceremony time comes, then we come together,
> we come together, have ceremony for one people,
>   Rirratjiŋu,
> a religion, the special ceremony,

Opposite left: *Bark painting by Wandjuk Marika, 1982.*

"The sunrise is coming up and all the lines towards it and up that's the ray, or reflection, the rays of the sun. When the sun is up the scrub turkey feeds himself. There is the line on each side of the painting which is the first food or grass, the little nut seeds the bustard likes himself, and on the bottom there's the goanna. The goanna is looking up the sunrise because in the night he was very cold, and the goanna came up and dried himself on the sun. All the sun rays and the sand is falling down as the goanna is crawling up and dry himself and also the bustard is doing the same thing." – Wandjuk Marika, 1984.

Opposite right: *Bark painting by Wandjuk Marika, 1982.*

As the sun sets, the goannas return to their home. The female Djanda is going into the entrance of their home beneath the large rock at Yalaŋbara. During the day, the dune sands blow across, obscuring the entrance.

---

3   Dhurryurrŋu – the name can now be spoken.

27

singing, dancing, burial, initiation and funeral,
all that circle is going through teaching young people.
We own two separate places.
It's one large area, sunset on the other side around the bay,
sunrise on the open sea, Yalaŋbara.

Djaŋkawu land first on that area, Yalaŋbara; and then went through.
My father was been teaching me where is Miliḏitjpi land, Miliḏitjpi
owned, also my grandfather, Djuwakan, and also the brothers
Marika, one is my brother's name (as I said earlier, can't call his
name) and also Djawuḻu, and the eldest son is Djuwakan – my
grandfather's boys – one mother one father, and they divided up into
every different area.

Yalaŋbara beach.

Now I have an auntie, my father's sister, Minirrki, her name is
Minirrki. She is still alive and she is always pushing me hard, to look
after Miliḏitjpi. But there is something – particularly the mining
company coming around here – ruining everything, run around with
vehicles on the hills down and spoiling good beach.
> My father taught me, he always tell me, "This is the land,
> our land,
> this is the land belong to different group;
> this is the land belong to different tribe."
> If you want to go this land (or the different tribe) you have
> to get permission
> but everybody knows, all the Yolŋu know,
> all the Aboriginal people know which is the part we own,
> the different area.

Yes I was been working with the Balanda, I didn't know where to go,
how to operate, in the Balanda world but I was been working, I was
been too busy on the white society. I try to civilise, to teach, to learn
more the Balanda way and also I learn more about my own culture,
my own totem or life from my own people, from my own father. He is
the wise man, he always take us that place. He take me always to
Yalaŋbara, go there walking, not like today driving in vehicle or four
wheel truck or Toyota, but we used to go round with the canoe, and
walk, walk through the bush, to all parts.

My father used to took me to the different area through the bush,
show me the places, which is not developed, which is far to go,
which is a special area, which is **where you can go through.** When
you travel you have to be very careful, not go to very important
place, no one ever allowed to go to that area, that special area or special ground.

> Now, I finish go through all this Balanda business,
> and I travelling every part of the world.
> I had enough.

I have to do what I want to do,
teach the people my own children
and **show** them because every tribe is concerned about that
    most important place, Yalaŋbara.
Yalaŋbara is higher and first.
Every places – like western Arnhem Land.
Every Yolŋu said to me,
I have to go stay looking after it because Yalaŋbara is
    the place,
Yalaŋbara is the creation.
Yalaŋbara is the first, most important place.
I have to stay looking after, not going to move away.

The rays of Walu, the sun, touch the Ancestors.

29

BEGINNING MY LIFE STORY

NOTES

Wandjuk recorded his memories in short bursts on visits to Sydney. His accounts followed his thoughts and mood at the time and the "story" was not necessarily sequential. In the book, to help the reader, and with the help of his family, the passages have been put into a sequence which roughly coincides with their occurrence in his life.

During the years (1974–87) that he was writing his life story, Wandjuk visited me in Sydney and stayed with my family while he did his work. For whole mornings he sat in a sunny room with tape recorder in hand while the Sydney lorikeets (sacred Rirratjiŋu birds) screeched loudly at the window. He alternated between his thoughts of past times, his message for the future, and conversations with the lindirritj.

Manymak (OK), today is Friday, January 27th, 1984 and I'm starting to give you something about my life story beginning with where I was born and how I grew up and learn about many things from my father and mother.

> I was born on a little island called Dhambaliya
> which is Bremer Island.
> I grew up in bush
> and learn all about what my father taught me
> and my mother taught me.
> My mother was for cooking bush food
> and father was for hunting,
> and at the same time he took me to the bush and was
>   teaching me
> about the creation, land creation,
> about the animals and the food, what to eat, what not
>   to eat,
> what to get, which is the right food,
> which is the wrong food – that we are not allowed to eat,
> which is the very important special food
> which is only for the elders
> not for the young people.
>
> Also he taught me about the land,
> who owned the land, what part of the different tribe owned
>   the land,
> and also he taught me things about my tribe or my religion,
> where they came from, where their land is,
> how we are divided up into Dhuwa and Yirritja.
> He told me about the many way and teach me.
>
> I learn about the song,
> I learn about the dancing,
> the special dance and sacred song and sacred implements.

30

I was been grow in the bush to be well and fit
and he taught me about where to go, how to live, what
    to find.

When I became about 15 years of age he taught me
how to hunt for
turtle –
go out in the sea, see which turtle right one to kill
and I was learn how to use the turtle spear, turtle rope
    and harpoon.
I learnt where is the good place to hunt the turtle for
    battling in the sea.
Also most important,
he taught me about the Wawilak and Djaŋkawu creation
    story.
I learn where to go,
what part of the country my own people own,
which part other people own the land,
like Gumatj, Maŋgalili, Djambarrpuyŋu, Madarrpa, Djapu,
    Gälpu, Ŋaymil and all the others.

*Mawalan Marika, Wandjuk's father,
Raŋi beach camp, Yirrkala, 1959.*

My mother's mother came from western Arnhem Land and my
father's mother's mother came from Groote[4] to Gaŋgan, to marry one
of the Dhalwaŋu people and then not long ago, a couple of years
back, my father's mother's brother passed away (which is my grandfather), and my father's father (which is my grandfather), he was passed
before I was born, and then my father was taught by my grandfather
and his father was taught by his great grandfathers coming for years,
story for centuries and centuries, generation to generation.

Now I **know**,
I know right now,
where to go, what to find, how to teach,
how to paint, what the story I am doing.
This is my life story and I can go through the bush
    by myself,
so I can find more courage, more power.

---

4   Groote Eylandt.

NOTES

Wandjuk Marika was considered the keeper of the Source of the Yolŋu "Book of Genesis". Yalaŋbara was the first landing place of Djaŋkawu. Wandjuk claimed direct lineal descent over many generations as eldest son of eldest son from Djaŋkawu, the Creation Ancestor himself.

Here Wandjuk gives a very brief explanation of the Djaŋkawu creation story. For Yolŋu all over north-eastern Arnhem Land, the Djaŋkawu (the brother and his two sisters) were responsible for the creation of half of all life – people, waterholes, sacred trees, plant sources. All Yolŋu are divided into two groups – Dhuwa and Yirritja, who intermarry. All the Dhuwa clans who now live throughout eastern Arnhem Land are descended from the original procreative acts of the Djaŋkawu. Wandjuk's responsibility was to uphold the law, keep the sacred sites and in particular supervise ceremonies decreed by Djaŋkawu for Yolŋu.

The Creation Ancestors arrived in

their canoe at Yalaŋbara on the coast of Arnhem Land and proceeded to travel west. Wandjuk Marika was the custodian of their landing place among many other sites. The songs and ceremony for most major Yolŋu ceremonies needed his input.

This version of the story is not the manikay – the song, the religion. He does not impart the detailed religious knowledge that was his great power. Much earlier in his life he and his father Mawalan had shared some of this with anthropologists. Today songs and ceremonial knowledge of Djaŋkawu are considered profound Yolŋu knowledge and property. As Wandjuk was aware that this book would be used by children he did not wish to go into more detail here but to simply place the Djaŋkawu in context so that all could understand his life, and his purpose.

The term Djaŋkawu can sometimes be confusing. It is the name used for the brother and also the combination of brother and two sisters – the three

creators combined. They were each creative in their own right, however the sisters have independent names mentioned in the text. There is also continuity and overlap between the travels of the Djaŋkawu and those of the Wawilak sisters whose journeys and creative acts extend further into central Arnhem Land. Wandjuk calls the Wawilak "children of Djaŋkawu".

Djaŋkawu activities set the pattern of behaviour for modern Yolŋu life. The appearance of the wulma, the thunderhead clouds, once indicated the time to move camp and travel inland for hunting. As the monsoon approaches, it is time to leave the coast where food will soon be difficult to get.

Wandjuk also briefly recounts how the Djaŋkawu came across the great spirit ancestor of the opposite moiety, the Yirritja, in the form of Banatja, standing where the wulma was touching the ground in a place called Banali. Banatja (or Laintjuŋ) holds an equivalent position in Yirritja philosophy as Djaŋkawu does for the Dhuwa.

DJAŊKAWU – CREATION STORY

This is my own stories I am writing what I know from my father. When I was about 15 years old he teaching me many thing before he pass away in 18-11-67, about 19 years now.

I am artist and song man and teacher for the maḏayin (sacred ceremony). When my father was pass away then I taking his places now. I am working as my father used to be – the stories about Djaŋkawu and Wawilak. Wawilak is two sisters and Djaŋkawu have two sisters again. Djaŋkawu, the brother and the two sisters.

> They were travelling through the seas for 40 days and
>   40 nights.
> then they landing at Yalaŋbara,
> they first landed at that place.
> Yalaŋbara.
> The two Wawilak sisters is children of Djaŋkawu, and his
>   two sisters Maḏalatj and Bitjiwurrurru.
> They landing at Yalaŋbara on the mainland.
> They came across the sea from Burralku Spirit Island or land
> and they staying at Yalaŋbara for 12 months.
> They naming the places and animals and they make
>   children or tribe
> what we call Malayaraŋu –
> Rirratjiŋu tribe, Ŋaymil, Darduyui, Djambarrpuyŋu, Djapu
>   and Gälpu including other tribes.
> That's why we are different tribes and different languages
> but we can understand each other.

> Then Djaŋkawu made a song – two kinds, sacred song and
>   public song.
> And then they start move toward Arnhem Bay
> because they saw the wulma, the rising thundercloud,
> the beginning of the wet season.

Bark painting by Wandjuk Marika.

Djaŋkawu walked across the land with his mawalan, sacred walking sticks. This painting coincided with the Land Rights case, a time when Djaŋkawu and the fight to protect his land was always on Wandjuk's mind.

Opposite: *The canoe the Djaŋkawu Creation Ancestors paddled to Yalaŋbara still rests on the sand among the waves. This sacred rock is called Guluwurru.*

Yalaŋbara sand dunes, the source of all creation.

And then the two sisters ask Djaŋkawu
"Shall we follow that cloud there, which is west – the sunset."
Brother said "OK, come. If we go through the bush you
    have to sing first about that cloud."

"Nhäŋa wulma dhäyan Borkinyaya
There is wulma the cloud, the rising at Borkinyaya

Nalim ŋarranŋan yappa gurrwundhuna
We are walking sister with our walking stick

Ŋupan ŋwuna wulma Ganyuŋuniyala yu
And follow that cloud over to Ganyuŋuniyala

Ma ngali ŋarruŋan."
We are going now over there.

Then they moved across the bush naming every animal
    they found –
djanda – the goanna, mayaya – frilled lizard, walmurrmurr
    or buwaṯa – plains turkey, maŋirrigirri – black flying fox,
and sang about them, giving them their names.
But every time they found animals they always asked brother
"What shall I do" –
Brother named them and started singing
Rainbow lorikeet – ḻindirritj, our totem.
Rirratjiŋu totem – maḏayin, sacred.
And then they found a little food (thin long shoots with
    special leaves)
grow in the ground they named Gomili (my son's name).
Their walking stick is called Mawalan (my father's name,
    and now my oldest son's name).
They reached a place called Gomiŋinybuy,
named because they saw the whistling ducks there in
    the billabong.
They were camping there for a month,
that's the Ŋaymil place.
Here they changed from Rirratjiŋu to Ŋaymil and that's
    Ŋaymil country today.

Then they saw another wulma at Gambuka,
which is Gälpu country.
As they walked toward there, they reached the place
and saw geese – gurrumaṯṯji,
and also put the djuta there – the special tree (from a
    walking stick).
Today we still see this tree – nobody can touch, cut or sit
    down there –
only my people can sit down there.

Because that place is madayin for my people, my
    father's father.
Then they went on further back to Gurunda
where they settled down for a while – put all the sacred
    objects there
and named it and put the djuta there.
Saw djanda and lindirritj (the rainbow lorikeet) and
    black flying fox (manirrigirri)
and the wild turkey (buwata).
Every animal they saw, the sister asked the brother
    for naming.
Nhä dhanum wäwa – "What is this brother?"
"Dhuwan ma djanda. That is a goanna.
Ma nali miyamana. Let us make a song."

Nha nälingu dhangu djanda
Hey! There's a goanna

Narrung dunu-walapum naraka muta
Crawling on the special tree (djuta) mutamurra

Then they left Gurunda and followed another wulma to
    Bilirri hills,
placed the sacred objects there, made the hills, formed them
and created the special food which is my son's name Gomili –
the root which is prepared by the women and eaten at
    special ceremonies.
Then they went off again to Bokinya
planted their digging sticks and palm trees grew which
    bear nuts –
tree name is Gulwirri.
Today my people collect these,
soak them for six days and then grind them into flour
    for eating.
They settled down there for a couple of weeks
then they travelling through the bush towards Naymil
    place,
reached a place called Gominyinbuy because here they saw
    the whistling ducks.
The same thing wherever they go,
the sister always asks Djankawu namings and groupings.

Now you have read this much and you know the story so far. I will tell
you the inside secret about the sisters…probably they are his wives.

This is the most important thing – something might be happening to
me but that word will be going into the story and our young people
will be surprised. That why I am putting it in my last story. We never

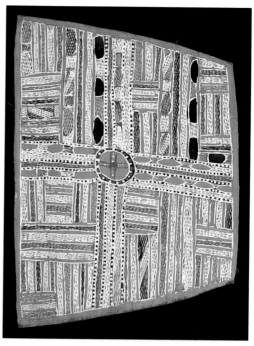

Bark painting by Wandjuk Marika, 1979.
Milngurr: the sacred place of fresh water.

*The circle represents the waterhole, sacred
fresh water under salt water, we call it
Milngurr. It represents the knowledge of
human beings like myself and the cross
means it represents north, east, south and
west, the four corners of the earth. Inside the
sacred waterhole Milngurr, when men drink
from Milngurr their hair turns grey. This is
Djankawu's waterhole. It tastes fresh and
different, fresh water is underneath and salt
water is on top, right out in the sea. When
the Djankawu were travelling on the sea
from Burralku, suddenly up came a freshwater spout and threw them to the beach.
The two sisters were thrown out and they
landed there. I drank that water that my
father showed me and that's how I got my
beard, grey hairs – no one else but me has
dived to that place and drunk the water.
One day soon I will show my grandson.*

*This painting is under the floor of the ocean
and all the little lines mean the clear water
and cloudy water mixed – or fresh and salt
water together. The black things represent
the trepang and the yellow ones same. The
trepang that don't have hatching on them are
under the muddy water. – Mawalan Marika
(Wandjuk Marika's son).*

told anthropologists that story, very special and important and only for the elders. The elders are the men who have the knowledge, experience, the ceremony and the song and grey hairs.

> Then they went to Marthi (Arnhem Bay)
> where there is a beautiful lagoon covered in waterlily,
> dhatam (leaves) or dhuŋu (roots).
> Biwudalmi – flowers of waterlily.
> They sang the song about them.
> That song belongs to Gälpu people,
> because they are the owners of dhatam.

> When they sang the song they saw a water snake coming up
>   from the lagoon.
> The snake's name was Ŋurrpanwa, or Djaykuŋ, or Dhunyin
> then they made a song about it, Gälpu song.

> While they were singing they saw the wulma at Banali.
> They travelled towards to where the cloud was standing.
> When they were getting closer they heard Banatja.
> He was standing in the middle of the road
> then the sister asked the brother, "Who is this man brother?"
> Then the brother said, "That is Banatja."
> Now this is what I know.

When I was young boy my father who was a very important man in Arnhem Land started to teach me the beliefs and ways of my people the Rirratjiŋu, the songs and dances and ceremonies and he also passed on to me his skill at playing the yidaki or didjeridu. My father knew all the designs or the stories of our ancestors and he showed me how to paint these. In this way I learnt from my father all the important thing I need to know about life, about our history, our customs and our ceremonies. When I lost my father I am the man responsible for keeping alive the songs and ceremonies and the stories and for passing them on when the time comes,

> The first people came to land at Yalaŋbara
> and they travelled across the country,
> they formed the mountains, rivers and waterholes.
> They created the different clan groups, by giving birth to
>   many children
> which are divided into Dhuwa and Yirritja moieties
> and made the skinships and marriage laws
> which are still followed today.
> They made the laws about initiation
> and about relationships between the different tribal groups
>   which is divided into Dhuwa and Yirritja.

Bark painting by Wandjuk Marika and his father Mawalan Marika, 1957.

Djaŋkawu creation story.

Djaŋkawu gave birth to the people at Yalaŋbara. Wandjuk's panels (second from the top and at the bottom) show the sisters with all their children and the afterbirth. The four circular patterns are the woven mats they covered themselves with while giving birth. Mawalan's panels (top) show the two sisters at left, and Djaŋkawu in a sacred shade at Yalaŋbara; his third panel again shows the Djaŋkawu in a creative act and depicts sacred waterholes and djuta.

Since the Dreamtime or Dreamland we have followed the
  customs and laws
that were made by the ancestors and we have kept sacred
  the special places
where important events took place
and where the first people finished their earthly journeys
  and became spirits.

These are sacred places to us and they remind us of the people and of
the laws they made. My Dreamland, Yalaŋbara – Port Bradshaw –
that's where they first settled down. We are very proud to mention
the name of the two sisters and we are proud of and believe in our
culture. We don't forget about our Dreamland. These two sisters
came from the island called Burralku. They travelled until they came
to Yalaŋbara which is Port Bradshaw.

Bark painting by Wandjuk Marika, 1982.
The birth of the children of Yalaŋbara.

*"You can see Djaŋkawu holding two sticks,
mawalan, two different mawalan which I
also take to the Land Rights Council to
show, to explain to the Land Rights case,
and on his chest the dilly bag is hanging.
The dilly bag he carried, not only he, but
the two sisters carrying them also, also the
mat, six mat. They used to carry the people
in these mats. Whenever they were ready to
create the people in a different area with
different languages of different clans, they
used to open up the mat and that means
those two sisters were the creators. This is
the two sisters. See these two sisters, they
created people and on top of this picture is
the brother walking towards sisters with
those two walking sticks or mawalan, which
is also my father's name, Mawalan. Those
two walking sticks turn into a tree, a
she-oak tree, you can see the male and
female the two sisters created. Djaŋkawu
is the brother.*

*The two sisters are there on the bottom of
this painting. They open up their leg there
and created all the people. On the bottom
of this painting, is six mats. The sisters
were covering themselves with the six mats
while they were creating the people. They
were covering themselves so their brother
won't be able to see, because in the Yolŋu
law, Aboriginal law, we not allowed to see
them having a baby. They have to be away
from brothers. The brothers must not know
what they're doing, but this is what they
have been doing. The mats, six of them, see
the little dots there, all the dots, that's the
afterbirth of the child or children as the
women know, but I am not allowed to say
this word. It is a special story and special
painting, I can say this. This is the painting
I translate only for Yalaŋbara, the most
important one, the most important painting." – Wandjuk Marika, 1984.*

NOTES

By the age of 18, Wandjuk had been through extensive ceremonial training and had been required to learn huge bodies of interconnecting knowledge – geography, song cycles, ceremonial management, protocol, multiple languages – as well as detailed survival and hunting techniques. The primary ritual obligations relating to Rirratjiŋu land came from his father. He also inherited rights to his father's mother's cultural heritage – the Dhalwaŋu Gumana group's songs, and in addition his mother's Warramiri songs. He retained all this, together with complete organisational and ceremonial information and the complex symbolic patterns and paintings that visually explained the ceremony and the land.

Wandjuk also mentions Woŋgu, a most powerful and feared leader of north-east Arnhem Land. The early colonial Northern Territory documents marvel at the number of wives he had and at his warlike ways. His was one of the earliest families to "settle" close to the emerging Methodist mission. Wandjuk learnt how to paint Macassan boats from Woŋgu. Indonesian fishermen had been visiting the coast of north-east Arnhem Land for centuries, hunting for trepang (sea slug). Their seasonal camps were set up near available natural water supplies and in some areas they dug deep fresh water wells. Today many beaches and wells are edged with large tamarind trees which grew from seeds discarded by these early visitors. The language and ceremony have many references to the Macassans, including the long-stemmed pipes, the use of flags in funeral ceremonies symbolising the departure of the soul like sails unfurling from Macassan boats, and ancient songs recounting the departure of ships across the seas. In his early youth Wandjuk was told stories by several older men of their visits on these boats back to Indonesia as crewmen for the Macassans, and scenes of their travels are depicted in bark paintings.

CEREMONY, DILLY BAG, TOTEM ANIMALS

Now, the most important teaching or training is in the ceremony. When I was very young of course I had my circumcision ceremony.

When I was seven years old my father took me across the bush across the land, to Dhaliŋbuy or Arnhem Bay, which is Wangurri tribe's land and outstation for the Wangurri group. Before, nothing was there when my father took me, only the bush. The people who live there they make a ceremony to make me a young man and they teach me more about the Law.

Then later on I was going through the Gunapipi (sacred initiation ceremony). It was big ceremony from Arnhem Bay. (They have homeland centre there, today, at Dhaliŋbuy.) They had a big ceremony there about the Gunapipi and my father took me to that area, Dhaliŋbuy, and they put me through Gunapipi.

My father went away. I was away from my parents for 18 months, and I did not see my mum and dad until my father and mother collected me there [at Dhaliŋbuy]. They get me there, because they were very worried, because I am their **eldest son** before my sisters and my brothers.

During Gunapipi I stayed there with a group of relations, all young men, which is my mother's tribe, for 18 months in the bush. We were the young men together going through learning for the cultural initiation ceremony for 18 months.

Then I **knew** all about life in the bush, how to behave. Do not touch anything, or muck around with anybody, or say bad words or swear, or make fun with other – don't just play around with the other people. I had to learn the right behaviour and to be a sensible, kind, respectable man. I study until I grew up to be a man.

Wuyula's circumcision ceremony. Wandjuk is smoking a luŋiny, long Macassan pipe.

Opposite: *The sacred memorial djuta is hung with many feathered dilly bags, string bags and strings of lindirritj feathers.*

Yes, I went to the Gunapipi when I was about 18 years of age for 18 months with the other people. Then my father and mother come to get me. They take me walk through the bush for two days (one night, two days), and then they meet the other people and then they make a decision to free me out from that ceremony. My mother and father said, "OK, we need our son to come home. Make him free so we can take him home, because we worry about him. He is our only son; he is a dear son to us." That what my parents were saying. Two days later we had a big ceremony, painted up ourselves with some kind of a paint, not a paint, a special thing.

I'm not going to say it.
If I say these words this book will spread out everywhere
and some Yolŋu people today they read and write
and if they read that word,
what I could say?
They will be coming to destroy me, all my family.
It is a very special word that I'm not going to say.
I'm **allowed** to say
but the book will be spread out **too** far
not only the south part of Aboriginal but the top part.
I can say these words, but I am careful of myself
because there are **so many dangers in Yolŋu life** or
      Yolŋu law.
Some of our laws are happy and some of them dangerous.
Even if the Aboriginal women, Yolŋu miyalk, know them,
      they not allowed to say them.

Aboriginal women are allowed to say only **main** words or common words, not the deep, dangerous special words. Even Aboriginal women, know or say word madayin, not raŋga (ceremonial object). The Aboriginal women are not allowed to say raŋga, only madayin. Many books use this one – yätj (bad) to see raŋga written down. All my people, we read together the story in books by people or the anthropologists. We thought that raŋga word was the most important, most dangerous, but today all my people worry about this raŋga word being used in public. These anthropologists show us no respect.

Funeral of Dhuŋdhuŋa, the first wife of the Dhanbul council chairman Roy Marika, in 1985. Women relatives await the arrival of the dancers at the funeral shelter. Wandjuk Marika played a central role in most funeral ceremonies.

Yes. After my parents took me back to Yirrkala
from the Gunapipi at Dhaliŋbuy,
my father made up his mind to make a big ceremony to
      teach me more
about the Djaŋkawu and Wawilak,
story, and dancing, and singing, and painting – all sorts
      of things.
Not only that, the Warramiri ceremony was on and my
      mother's tribe was there too – octopus and flying fox
      people.
They have a responsibility to teach me at the same time as
      my father is teaching me about our own law and
      ceremony and song.

Now, today, I have so much knowledge about ceremony,
  song, not just my own.
I have two songs – my own songs and my mother's songs –
  including Marrakulu song, Gälpu song; and also Djapu.
And the sacred inside ones, maḏayin,
and also the paintings.
I also know their painting because old Woŋgu was
  teaching me their painting.
A good painter. He painted Macassan boats and also his
  own painting.
And then I know Gumatj bottom, Gumatj top, two groups,
Gumatj Yunupiŋu, and Gumatj Yarrwidi.
It's one group, divided into three, Burarrwaŋa, Yarrwidi
  and Yunupiŋu.
And also I learnt the paintings of Ŋaymil and
  Djambarrpuyŋu and Ḏätiwuy
and my father's tribe,
and also my father's mother's tribe, like the Dhaḻwaŋu
  Gumana.
There is two parts of Dhaḻwaŋu – Gumana (my father's
  mother) and Wunungmurra.

So, I had Djaŋkawu
and all these.
And I learnt it all.

*The dancers enter the shade and approach
the funeral shelter.*

How could I learn all that? Well, that's a good question. Because I'm
the top man's son. Because my father is the most important man. He
has more experience, he has more knowledge from his father, my
father's father – because – I have many generations before me including the main one, Djaŋkawu our creation. We are the sons who know
how to make, where to go, where to find the place.

It was my father who drew up and marked out which is the dancing
places for public ceremony and which is dancing place only for the
men. The ceremony, special ceremonies for men only are in the bush.
We were dancing there, I was learning there, early hours of the morning, singing. Then we come out to the public where everyone is
painting. Men, women, children, girls and boys waiting in a big circle. If you see the film *Memory of Mawalan*, my father, you see the
ceremony, the same. I have the stick, walking stick, pointing out
that's where he lived. **He** made that ceremony, to go **through**,
because his time was coming near. He brought that special djuta-stick
into the special ceremony to teach me to use it for public, as well as
sacred men's ceremonies. He drew up which is the dancing for public,
which is dancing only for the man. We have the two, for both
Wawilak and Djaŋkawu ceremonies, one is only for the men, one for
the public. In the public ceremony everybody dances, circles around

as the two sisters have been doing, trying to stop the snake come near. The snake was coming towards them stronger and stronger, at last it swallowed baby and baby's mother.

Then the same thing for Djaŋkawu ceremony also.
In Djaŋkawu there are special ones also only for the man,
and then we come out from the special site
walking toward the public area
towards the woman dancing.
Then they (the women) **mix** with the man
because Djaŋkawu and his two sister have been travelling
   through the bush.

The Rirratjiŋu have the sacred animals. If you, Balanda, are
   coming to top end of Australia, then you should know
   about this.
Because too many are hunting our Creation, our animals,
and they don't know anything, what it means.
What the land means
and **who** the animal **is**.
Well, I tell you here in this my book.

Wandjuk Marika directs the participants at the ceremony. He was known as the yindi buŋgul for funerals.

Opposite: *The funeral shelter.*

The l̲indirritj is sacred and very important, special to my people. L̲indirritj, (rainbow lorikeet), yes, the most important bird for Rirratjiŋu, Ŋaymil, D̲ät̲iwuy, Boyuyukululmi, Djambarrpuyŋu people. That's the most important totem for us all, but we not allowed to kill that bird. We have to go to some other people, or nearby relations to go and shoot the l̲indirritj for our feathers. We always make sacred objects for the ceremonies and we use l̲indirritj feathers. We still make dilly bag, not men but the women. Men work on the feather string to put with the dilly bag – it's a very important thing. Used to be my Auntie, my father's sister, who made all the sacred dilly bag. Now my first wife, she makes all the dilly bags, the special ones for ceremony. I am always organising for dilly bag for ceremonies. Usually they going to make one in Gan̲gan̲, different style or differ-ent l̲indirritj feathers.

We used to have the big ceremonies while it's dry, nothing any rains – before the rain. When I go back home I will do the ceremony, the dilly bag ceremony, to teach the young people, my own people, my own tribe, including my children. I have to teach everyone, not only my own tribe, but I have to bring people from different areas, also from Elcho Island.

That dilly bag is the Djaŋkawu dilly bag. It is very important thing and we are not going to lose that.

*Banduk Mamburra Marika and Gayili
Marika at the funeral ceremony.*

The young girls are learning to make the special dilly bags
not only special dilly bags,
but all sorts of dilly bags – ordinary dilly bag for dancing,
or for hunting to collect some ŋatha (food) or maypal
    (shellfish) or whatever.
The dilly bag are all made from pandanus, the feathers are
    always just lindirritj.
They are not killed at home, always somewhere else, so I
    won't be able to see it. I only see the feathers,
but not how they treated the bird or shoot them
because it's my sacred bird, my totem bird.
Another clan, not my own clan, gets them.
For, if we kill our own relative or totem we get sick.
The Djaŋkawu rule,
He say, "Yaka, do not kill anything
even the bustard, the plains turkey, the buwata."
We are not allowed to kill that one, buwata.
We're not allowed to kill djanda (goanna) or any other
    Dhuwa animal.
There are two kinds of djanda,
the Yirritja have spots everywhere and yellow tail,
but Dhuwa djanda is all black.
If you see these Dhuwa goanna you are not allowed to kill,
if you see the Yirritja you can kill for your food.
If you see buwata on the road when you are driving, you are
    not allowed to shoot.
There are many at Yalaŋbara,
so many,
goanna and buwata.

All the time we are driving all the children see
    these animals.
They say,
"Look, look, look, buwata, buwata."
I think the buwata know, they feel safe.
And also goanna the same too.
He is always just crawling across the road,
or sometimes he is lying there on the roadside while the
    truck is going past.
More further towards Yirrkala they are around there
    somewhere,
you can kill those goanna at Yirrkala, but not the buwata.
Even Yirritja people are also not allowed to kill their totem,
like the huge red kangaroo or emu or the bandicoot.
The Dhuwa echidna we are not allowed to kill.
The Yirritja clan are not allowed to kill emu, kangaroo,
    yellow belly snake or the crocodile.

We used to be able to kill crocodiles, but now we are
  not allowed.
If Dhuwa moiety need crocodile we have to ask.
If we kill without permission they will charge us money
  this time,
but it used to be all free,
free to go, free to hunt.

That dilly bag is very important to our people.
The sacred dilly bag is part of the ceremony,
and part of the sacred objects.
It is made from the sacred feathers.
That's the story about this dilly bag, the sacred dilly bag.
When the girls, or women, finish it, everything fixed, everything ready to use,
then we make a big ceremony,
singing about the Djaŋkawu.

*Climax of the manikay at the memorial
ceremony some years after the death of
Wandjuk's father Mawalan. Wandjuk
Marika and his younger brother are
standing at the left.*

CROCODILE HUNTING

NOTES

Crocodiles were extensively hunted for their skins in the decades following the Second World War. Aborigines across the North used only traditional spears and a close understanding of the habits of crocodiles to kill and skin them safely. The work was hazardous however, and fatalities did occur. The mission at Yirrkala acted as a depot for the purchase and sale of crocodile skins.

Wandjuk still occasionally hunted crocodiles up until his appointment to the Aboriginal Arts Advisory Committee of the Australia Council for the Arts (1972).

The numbers of crocodiles decreased dramatically until they were protected under the law. With neither skin hunters nor Yolŋu culling them, their numbers increased dramatically. They can be found along most salt water beaches, inland rivers and billabongs across the Top End of the Northern Territory. Some hunting is now permitted.

When I finish the Gunapipi I go out again to Arnhem Bay to hunt for crocodile. So they can give us money. Maybe £3 or maybe £4 or maybe £100, for crocodile skins. We kill the crocodile with the spear, the three-pronged spear. I used to make the barbed spear. I used to sneak in while they lay there minding eggs, sneaking slowly with the fish spear, along the banks. There is water like a billabong, in from the river, and the crocodile used to crawl from the river to the billabong and lay their eggs there – hundreds of nests. We had to move quietly – these days they shoot them. And then one day my father was short of ŋarali (tobacco) and ŋatha (food). So we take the skin back, just walk one night, from Arnhem Bay to Yirrkala, sell the skins and get the ŋarali, and the next day we walk back again to Arnhem Bay.

Well, my father was painting and also he prepare for the ceremony, and also he was always with me to show me how to sneak in, how to hunt and keep an eye on me, and protecting me. Even though I was 20 years old, he protecting me from the danger, the crocodile. He show me where to catch him, how to sneak in behind him centrally on breakaway (never to make noise, sneak up silently) where they are laying their eggs on dry land. They lay their eggs and the mother crocodile is lying beside the eggs to protect them, and sometime they lie on top of the eggs in a sort of nest, and I used to be sneaking in. I had to be careful for watch out very closely for the tail whipping and I learn how to cut the hide, dry it up, carry back to Yirrkala. And then one month later, I do it my way and take all the young boys to do more hunting, show where to go – because I know where to go, I know how to hunt, how to find.

Yes, there was the crocodile, right on the Yirrkala billabong. We take the children up to the lagoon. We used to paddling with the canoe – that creek used to be one big area, but now they put the town there and a road across to the beach and now some of the trees dead. Now, the crocodile we hardly ever get but we can always see the track from

46

the salt water to the billabong. When wet season coming up, all the crocodiles is hatching out, the little ones, young ones about this time of the year. When the big rain come and wash everything sometimes the mother carry the young ones, all the little ones on the head – every little one on top from tail to head.

After, when I finished with the crocodile, then I was naughty – killed one cow at the mission camp and we eat and feed ourselves right in the bush jungle. But one dog, the missionaries' dog, male, he smell and he pick up the cowhide and he took that hide right up to where his owner was and handed it to the man. I think it was one of the Fijian ministers, Daniel Lotu, and he picked up this and then gather all the young boys and asking "Who did it?" I said I did and he was asking why I did it. "I was starving, because we didn't have food." "OK, Wandjuk six months labour." My father said, "OK, my son he not going to work. I'm going to take him to Bremer Island, for six months." And then I was staying on Bremer Island for 12 months, instead of six months, and I come back to Yirrkala, caught some turtle at Bremer Island. We took the turtle to Yirrkala beach to feed all the people – and that was 1951.

Crocodiles still come to Raŋi, the beach at Yirrkala where Wandjuk grew up.

The old lippa-lippa (dug-out canoe) he once used now rests near the family's shelter.

MASSACRE

Back to travelling – when I was a young man, my father took me, to Maŋgalili land, to Djapu land, At the same time there is a Balanda coming up from south, Bill Harney. I remember his name, he took the soldiers and drive them by their car – horses – through Arnhem Land.

> They try to shoot the people, the same thing they do in
>   South Australia, Western Australia, Victoria and in
>   some part of Sydney.
> They did the same thing to my people in Blue Mud Bay.
> They take the horses from Darwin by boat, landed in
>   Arnhem Bay
> try to kill all the people.
> I don't know why,
> they try to get the land near Biranybirany.
> Woŋgu's father brother – three Djapu and three
>   Djambarrpuyŋu.

And then all my mothers and father leave me on the street, good job nobody ever run over me by the horses. There is one man, who was working as a police tracker in Darwin for many years and also he is a part of my family, my mother's brother, and he recognise me and he pick me up and put me on horseback and then he asked me (I heard this from my mother) – ask me who I was, which my parents, who is my mother.

> I still remember this, I said to him, "My mother is sunset,
>   my mother is Bamatja",
> and that man was brother of my mother, his name is
>   Dhuritjini.
> He said, "OK I know – she is my sister."
> I said, "Where's my mother, I don't know where my mother
>   is."
> And he said to me, "OK, I am looking for her, and when I
>   find her I am going to hand you to her, to my sister,
> you're my son, my sister's boy, you need not worry.
> I look after you, for these people are working for me."

48

He was the leader. I think I was under eight years of age and he went to Caledon Bay.

Because my father, mother and my people used to travelling from place to place to protect the land, from Caledon Bay right up to where the town mining company township [is now] right up to Melville Bay, right round the Cape Wilberforce to Elcho Island, I still remember some of the people, Barrarrŋu, near Wessel Islands, and all my mother's tribe Warramiri, they used to travelling around many places, they meet each other to share the culture and to meet the people and to discuss many things.

NOTES

On 17 September, 1932, a group of Yolŋu camped at Caledon Bay killed several Japanese and looted their vessel. The killings were in retaliation for the Japanese abuse of Aboriginal women. There were some allegations at the time that Aboriginal men had colluded in making the women available but were angry at lack of payment. Two white beachcombers were also killed on Woodah Island for the same crime. On 1 August, 1933 Constable McColl, one of a police party sent to investigate the killings, was also speared to death at Woodah Island. The outcry among the white community in the Northern Territory about these killings demanded a punitive expedition to teach Aborigines a lesson. Church groups and others protested and so a "peace expedition" resulted, via the Anglican CMS (Church Missionary Society) which then had missions at Roper River and Groote Eylandt, close to the areas of the encounters.

The group went unarmed in order to establish peaceful relations before suggesting that the killers give themselves up. It was an attempt to prevent police killing the whole Caledon Bay community. They travelled with Aboriginal assistants in the wet season of 1933–34 to Caledon Bay and eastern Arnhem Land in the mission lugger *Holly*. They easily located via word of mouth the Aboriginal "murderers" and persuaded them to go back to Darwin. The three Aborigines were found guilty of killing the Japanese and were given 20 years hard labour. Two of them were Tukiar and Merara. Tukiar was sentenced to death but was later released; he disappeared almost immediately and no trace was ever found of him. The rumour was that the police had murdered him in retaliation for killing one of their own.

The case was a tragic miscarriage of justice based on an original aggressive act on Aborigines' own land. Tukiar's trial was a miscarriage of justice as he had not been arrested but had travelled to Darwin freely to give an explanation, assuming that right and justice was on his side owing to the nature of pay-back and self-defence in traditional law as well as protecting Aboriginal women from these increasingly frequent interlopers who acted violently and arrogantly.

It is not clear from Wandjuk's memories how his early experiences connect to these incidents. Yolŋu oral histories mention shootings and a person remembered as responsible is 'Bilarney', but this Bill Harney is not to be confused with the famous outback Australian writer of the same name.

NOTES

Fishermen from the Macassan Straits in Indonesia had been visiting the northern coast of Australia for centuries, mainly collecting trepang. Exactly how long this had been going on remains the subject of considerable research and dispute. It was a sufficiently long period for aspects of Indonesian culture to enter Yolŋu language, custom and ceremony. Although his father and grandfather had told him of the Macassans and indeed worked with them when they set up camp in the bays in north-east Arnhem Land, the incident of finding coins on the beach described by Wandjuk marks the beginning of his connection to the wider world. Along the beach camp Raŋi where Wandjuk lived with his family and where his sister Mamburra, her children and other family members now live, there are now huge tamarind trees grown from seeds brought by the Macassans. In common with other men of his generation, Wandjuk always kept with him a long pipe (luŋiny), reminiscent of Indonesian smoking implements, the

shaft of which was always painted with ochres, sometimes with Rirratjiŋu cross-hatched patterning.

The stick tobacco given by the missionaries as payment for various tasks was replaced with tin or packet "Drum" tobacco as the pipe accompanied Wandjuk throughout his life on travels, performances, speeches and during interaction with the wider international community.

Other features of Yolŋu life which are similar to Indonesian customs include the particular form of beard worn by some men: Mawalan, Wandjuk and now his eldest son, Mawalan. At funeral ceremonies, Macassan knives or "kris" are also held aloft, swirling and flashing. Many features of Macassan life appear in bark paintings of the 1950s and 1960s.

When in Sydney on Aboriginal Arts Board business, Wandjuk was astounded to see the engraved silver curved "swords" as he called them in

the window of a gun shop near Sydney's Central Railway Station. Along with purchasing feathers for ceremonies he spent his director's fees from the Aboriginal Arts Board on these Macassan swords to take home for ceremony. Towards the end of the first phase of funeral ceremonies, when the body is still in the shade before being taken to its final resting place, a farewell dance is performed in which flags are held aloft and waved. It is thought this practice entered Yirrkala and eastern Arnhem Land in ancient times due to the raising of the sails both on dugout canoes and departing Indonesian luggers, many of which took Aboriginal seamen aboard to work on the fishing expeditions.

The value Wandjuk gives to different coins are confused in his account. As he says, "I don't know what the money was worth." The difficulty for Yolŋu of Wandjuk's generation was compounded when Australia changed to decimal currency in 1966.

FINDING RUPIAH

We used to hunt in the place called Buymarr
and we stand there and get the turtles
and then hunting for the fish.
It was been for a long time, I don't know what year,
because I'm not thinking good enough in those days,
because I did not know anything about what beyond that,
    what coming.

One day we are selling turtle shells, spears and shells, nothing money like any we have today. We got only stick tobacco. We used to get it and cut it in half and sell it or they give us smokes, like the payment. We sell the pearl shell, or clam shell, or turtle shell, tortoiseshell, or anything like spear or rope or dilly bag. They used to give us stick tobacco, black tobacco, instead of money, and then I walk along. I didn't smoke by that time because I was a little boy.

I walk along the beach playing around, pick up many kind of drifting bottles, and I find a little tin, and I'm shaking it, and my mother was with me. Then I heard the rattling inside the tin, and I open it up and there's the penny, two penny, (used to be a penny before) and I open it and there's a penny, two penny, and I show it to my mother, "Hey, Mum, I found something which is the metal," and she said, "Come and show me," and I show her and she say, "Oh, that's a bulayi, rupiah that's the money," and I said, "What you going to do with it Mum?" And my Mum answer, "We'll try to take it to the missionary, to see whether it is the money or it is the bulayi." Macassan used to give this thing to Yolŋu for working, they used to work for Macassans, my father's father, Djuwakan, used to working for them and my grandfather and my father used to work on this one, and they, Macassans, used to give them this – bulayi or doi, and that why they get this name – rupiah, because the Macassan gave them this name, (but our own name is bulayi). Bulayi is a metal, doi is the money, rupiah is the money we use right now.

Collecting coral for sale at the mission, 1959.

Opposite: *Raŋi beach at Yirrkala, 1959.*

Wurrayana and the children outside the mission school, 1959.

Yirrkala creek, a favourite swimming place for children, 1959.

Then I polished it up, nice and shiny golden, and then gave it to the missionary, one of the missionaries. My mother asked, "Can you tell us this, is it doi or is it bulayi?" The missionary said, "No, this is the money. Today, we only gave you black stick, black tobacco, part of this money is exactly the same." He show us the money, "Penny" he said, "this is penny, this one penny, this two penny." And then he show us the money. "OK this is one shilling" (today is ten cents) and then he pick up the little one, which today is five cents, and five shilling is ten shilling and then he pick up two shilling – today we call twenty cents, "This is the two shilling" (that we call today twenty cents). And then he always counting up, adding up, and he said, "Here is a ten shilling" and then he show other shilling. "There's four shilling" (that is today forty cents) and then he pick up the little one, which is ten cents today. "OK put the two together", "OK," he said, "This is fifteen shilling (that we have $1.50). And then he show us the paper money – "OK this is the £1". We used to have £1, before, now we have $1, now we have a coin, golden coin. Today, we have golden coin for $1, and then he show us another £2 and put together £2, altogether £4, that we have $4, and we put £1 again, and we make £5, and that we have $5. I don't know what the money was worth.

And then money has been opened up – because I found that money in Winyinymarra, or Caledon Bay – I think the English name of it is Alexander Mountain. Yes, Mount Alexander, that's a Balanda name, and Yolŋu name of that place is Winyinymarra, where the money was open up.

Playing games at Yirrkala, 1959.

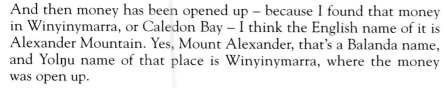

A shade built on the sands at Raŋi; the family was able to lead a cleaner and healthier life then as the creek was not polluted, 1959.

NOTES

This tale of such a long journey on foot has entered the statutes of "legendary acts" among young family members. The journey is unusual for the distance, but more so because of the historically hostile "country" or peoples the young men would encounter. To Yolŋu, the elements of courage against alien spirits and powers and survival achievements are stronger than the actual physical feat of travelling hundreds of kilometres on foot.

Wandjuk and the others were able to follow knowledge of communities and family/kinship connections through almost to Maningrida, as the Djaŋkawu and the Wawilak ancestors travelled that way too, leaving waterholes and making children. As Wandjuk says, "Wherever I travel I follow the serpent like snake, like Djaŋkawu and many more."

As Wandjuk recalls, when he finally returned to Yirrkala on a mission

ketch, there was work to be done – with anthropologists Ronald and Catherine Berndt in Yirrkala and continuing the translation of the Bible into Gumatj language. This translation (for Beulah Lowe of the Church Mission Society) was the first such translation in Arnhem Land.

WALKING TO DARWIN

Sometime I used to go through the bush myself for two days without no one so I can get the experience, and so I can know the knowledge about the nature, how we live, what my people used to do, where to go, where to find. Then how to learn.

Then after that, long after, when I was about 16 years of age, I testing myself, I take nine people with me. We tried to find the bush where I was grown, where I was learn. We walked from Yirrkala through the bush to Darwin. It taked us about 26 day and we walk through the bush, and sometime we find it hard to find any food or water. Three days no water, only food, but we know what to find in the bush. It was very dangerous – three days food, no water, after three, or five days just walkabout without water. And it was very tiring time all through the bush right up to Maynorru Station which is maybe 2, 4, 500 miles from Darwin and we were there for maybe a month and we meet the people there.

> Strange people
> but we know each other by the totem, by the mother's side,
> by the Creation which is their own Creation,
> their story, what their belief is, and we know each
>   other then.
> And then we called each other brothers and sisters.
> They had a big ceremony there, a special ceremony, a
>   sacred ceremony,
> and one of the old men, the head man of the ceremony
>   invited us
> to show us the sacred object,
> to take us and show us and tell us about the story,
> exactly the same story from east to south or wherever you
>   can go,
> and then I learn more about their ways.
> They have exactly the same story
> but different names,

Wandjuk's father Mawalan (standing) watches a gathering of singers accompanied by a yidaki player at Raṇi, 1959.

Opposite: *Wandjuk and his relatives walked through these forests of cycads near Ramingining and on through the rugged escarpment country of Arnhem Land.*

same story, same ceremonies, different language,
but we know each other by the totem, by the story,
by the culture, by the law.

We were there for a month and then they rang to Darwin. Today they are Aboriginal Affairs, but in those days Native Affairs. I think he is still alive that man, Ted Evans, Dr Copell and some others (I forgot their names) they were there. They thought we got lost, but we not lost, they pick us up and take us to Katherine and we were waiting there Katherine Hospital, and then we meet another people, another tribe, exactly the same thing – a story!

Wherever I been travel I follow the serpent like snake,
like Djaŋkawu and many more, and I know.
We sit together and they asking us
and they know their story is the same
and the skin totem is the proof they are the same as us.
Wherever you go we know each other by the totem
by the skinship –
maybe kangaroo, or snake or goanna or emu or sea hawk or
    eagle hawk –
and then you know
and then you call each other brothers and sisters.
Or what your skin – Balang...
and that what I have been learning, about the Yolŋu.

Wandjuk Marika, Professor R.M. Berndt and Muŋgurrawuy (Gumatj clan leader) crossing the old bridge from Raŋi to Yirrkala, 1968.

We were in Darwin for three months, then one of the fishing boats run by the missionaries in north Australia, Methodist mission (they run two boats, one is *Aroetta* and one is *Larrpan*). They pick us up there in Darwin and take us back to Yirrkala, and from then on I start working and learning all about it. There were 11 sacred sites through different clans' lands, but nobody had learned any English in those days.

Ronald Berndt was there, he was helping those people and he tried to find the man who speak English to translate the Yolŋu story. So, I was translate to him for the different clan including my own story, from my father, for Professor Berndt. At the same time my father he taught me many things, how to hunt, how to go, how to teach, not only that, but after I become a teaching assistant for the missionaries. Teach all the young people like Doŋga, Daymbalipu, like Wally Wulaŋbuma, and many more young people.

Now they are running their own way, but I was the man who went first, first teaching assistant for the missionaries; not only that but first for the whole Balanda system and the Yolŋu system, not only that, but at the same time I translated the Holy Bible to Yolŋu and from the Methodist hymn book translate to Yolŋu. We use that Bible today everywhere along the top part of Australia – Arnhem Land. I was the man, the first, the man to do that work.

Young children playing on the lippa-lippa canoe, Yirrkala, 1959.

Then I start to do paintings
and many Balanda coming
come in and go,
come and go.

Then I have a problem, a big problem coming up while my
    father was still alive,
and then he make the big ceremony about the Wawilak
    ceremony
(that has a film today),
and then I learnt more about Wawilak sacred object,
    song, dancing.
Then after that I was worried – he passed away in 1967
and I was very sad because I have lost my father.

Before he was passed away he taught me many things,
how to upright,
he learnt me to sing and carry, to lead the ceremony,
to teach the movement,
to teach the step by step, which is which,
my father was always watching.
Then we did many paintings together – all my painting is
    in Art Gallery of New South Wales.
Not only there but in many places.
This is my father and my painting,
all the sacred objects collected by Professor Berndt and
    some other individual anthropologists they had
    been visiting,
going about collecting, lots of painting,
lots of story, recording,
song,
then I was worry for a couple of years.

NOTES

Donald Thomson was an important ethnographer of Cape York and Arnhem Land. He is noted in particular for his exceptional photographic record of life in the 1920s and 1930s.

During the War, the northern coast of Australia was considered extremely vulnerable to Japanese attack. In order to safeguard the coast, a radical plan was developed by which Aborigines were to form the basis of a volunteer army over the entire area – creating a network of coastwatchers. Thomson was appointed to form this Aboriginal guerrilla force to defend the scattered airfields and provide intelligence. He had a ketch at his command, the *Aroetta*. Thomson's "crew" that Wandjuk mentions included Solomon Islanders, a Torres Strait Islander and Raiwalla, a Yolŋu man from the Glyde River area. Thomson's instructions were

> To gather together a small unit of the aborigines [sic] who possess special prowess in hunting, in craftsmanship and bushcraft, and who are skilled in guerrilla warfare and ambush, and to use these natives for the instruction of members of the Independent Companies in tropical bushcraft and in living on the resources of the country. [5]

Thomson had worked at Trial Bay among Yolŋu in the 1930s and knew Woŋgu and others. Many apparently offered to help. It was ironic that only ten years or so after several Yolŋu had been jailed for killing Japanese (at Caledon Bay), another team led by Thomson was attempting to convince them that they *could* really kill Japanese who landed in the Territory. However, as the Japanese had been landing intermittently on the coast and skirmishes, murders and mistreatment of women resulted in great animosity, the Yolŋu were happy to assist Thomson's endeavours.

Thomson apparently travelled barefoot[6] as he wanted the party's tracks to suggest the entire group was Aboriginal and that there was no European officer in command. He was also intent on impressing his Yolŋu "soldiers" with his adaptability. On training exercises elsewhere in Arnhem Land, he was renowned for an exercise involving a long night swim through a mangrove area, yet in Wandjuk's memory although he "walked strong" he appeared nervous, carried a map and sometimes "he slip and fall over". However his dog, Daga, was a hero because of his hunting prowess. When Wandjuk and his father reached a muddy river infested with crocodiles and sharks it was they who made a raft to "put that Balanda Donald Thomson on...and we are also crawling in mud, mud is right up to your knees." Thomson, who had an infected leg, recorded this event in his field notes:

> I was now holding the party back. Hitherto I had always been able to lead them and eventually tire them out. When we reached the river the prospect did not look attractive. It was a wide, muddy estuary lined, as usual, with a dense unbroken wall of green mangroves standing above a bank of grey mud. It was low water but there was still about eighty to a hundred yards to swim, and all these rivers are infested with crocodiles.
>
> The Aborigines now took the initiative. They collected the dry buoyant driftwood that lay about and lashed it together with strips of the green bark of the Cotton-tree (*Hibiscus tiliaceus*). This did not look very secure and as I could not hope to swim very far with my leg as it was, I took the straps off my canvas bag and strapped these around the bundle to supplement the bark. On top of this crude raft the men placed the sheets of tea-tree bark which they had obtained for the purpose, earlier in the morning, and stripping off my clothes I lay naked on top. The women remained on the bank and the men swam with me, pushing the raft across, while I paddled with my hands. They landed me safely on the north bank and then returned with the "raft" for the gear. [7]

According to army records, Yolŋu were not paid although sometimes they were issued three sticks of tobacco per week. In the bush they lived on bush tucker and were expected to find this themselves. Sometimes Thomson issued tomahawks, knives, fishing lines and so on. Thomson's unit was disbanded after 16 months of patrols and the security of Arnhem Land was largely entrusted to Yolŋu who theoretically remained alert to the Japanese threat. This was certainly the case for Wandjuk as he recounts in the next chapter the story of the plane crash on Bremer Island and his caution for fear the pilot was Japanese.

---

5   Robert A. Hall, *The Black Diggers*, Allen & Unwin, North Sydney, 1989, p. 92.

6   ibid, p. 97.

7   Donald Thomson, *Donald Thomson in Arnhem Land*, compiled by N. Peterson, Currey O'Neil Ross Pty Limited, Victoria, 1983, p. 64.

DONALD THOMSON

Now I go back again, to tell about the Dr Thomson, Donald Thomson. We family went by boat or travelling round with lippa-lippa to Yalaŋbara. School holiday with father's brother and sister's husband and family and all the family right round Cape Arnhem, right round and it took maybe two or three days. So we get the turtle, place to place, until we reached Yalaŋbara sunset side and then next day we saw the boat of Donald Thomson and he landed.

He talked to my father and he said to one of the young men, Rewara, "Try to fight the Japanese." Then he took some men. He said to my father, "Let's go through the bush, show me where this (Japanese) is coming from." English Company Islands Mata-Mata today, Gumatj, owned by my mother's Warramiri group, that was the area. My father said, "I know where to lead you, where to tell you."

And we travel exactly the same when I was walking, when I was four years old, I walked through with my father and Dr Thomson and all his crew. Also Galarrwuy's father had been on the boat travelling around so we had to wait for him at Cape Wilberforce on other side. We had to walk through the bush from Yalaŋbara toward Arnhem Bay – take us about roughly four week.

At the same time my father showed me food also he taught Thomson about poison food, many things about the sick medicine and the animal what we are allowed to eat. When I was young the emu and porcupine forbidden for me to eat – until I am become a man. And then I walk through the bush. He taught me many ways, not only the food he taught me, the name of the places, and name of the people which is that place. We walk through for two or three week.

> He taught me the tribes and what are the names of the
> places that belong to Ŋaymil, Wangurri, that belong to
> Dätiwuy and some other tribes.

Paperbark swamp near Yirrkala.

He said "This is so and so place,
part of Rirratjiŋu for example
Ŋaymil and Rirratjiŋu and Ḏäṯiwuy have same totem and
    same story about the Djaŋkawu."
This is why he taught me, so I can know.
That's what he taught me so I can know the places and
    the land.

All the land is the same, but their name is different.
It is simple,
a special kind of a tree, it is a symbol of the tribe.
This is from the Djaŋkawu
and more further, maybe you could see a rock or a lump
    of ground
and then he said, "This is for Wangurri."
The creek or the land country and the swampy area or some
    bird or some anything and you know it's the different
    people land
or there is a waterlily, dhatam, symbol of Ŋaymil
    and Ḏäṯiwuy
then you know there is the tree where Djaŋkawu turn into
    tree and establish the area,
the place where Djaŋkawu created the children – "Mätjarra"
Different but exactly the same – Rirratjiŋu, Ŋaymil,
    Ḏäṯiwuy,
also right up to Elcho Island exactly the same tribe,
    Mätjarra
which is a special tribe belong to Djaŋkawu children.
We are the children of Djaŋkawu.
Doesn't matter which part western Arnhem land, eastern
    Arnhem Land.
Western Arnhem Land all the way from Ramingining right
    up to Oenpelli
and from Milingimbi or Ramingining right up to where I
    am, is eastern Arnhem Land,
children of Djaŋkawu.

On Elcho, there's the Mätjarra, the Boyuyukululmi group,
    which is singing Djaŋkawu song,
the special song, like myself and my group, Rirratjiŋu,
we singing two or three singing about Djaŋkawu, we have a
    special song or special ceremony for the circumcision
and for the burial
and many more.
For the burial we are singing two or three songs (song
    sequences).
I mean, Djaŋkawu and Wawilak
and the Yirrkala songs which are seagull, or dhanbul,

The Djaŋkawu travelled across from Yalaŋbara to Ramingining where they made this sacred waterhole, looked after by the children of Djaŋkawu today.

The other like Marrakulu, Marraŋu have only one, like the
Wawilak song or Ŋaymil have the devil spirit song, the
devil spirit song.
If these have special ceremony for Djaŋkawu I'll have to
helping them.

Anyhow now we go back to the story. We walk and we travel. Dr
Donald Thomson he get worried. He always say to my father, "Hey,
you take me wrong place, where are we, where are we, how far we got
to go?" and my father he say, "Relax, just relax, we take you to the
place we got to go, where we heading for." Dr Donald Thomson walk
strong. It was dry season. Sometime he would wearing hat, I still
remember this. Yes, he took out the map, he took it out and crawling
like Yolŋu and sometime he's walking up the hill, mountain and
down, and sometime he slip and fall over and my father used to help
and he also had big dog called "Daga", like a lion, big **huge**. He used
to catch our food – dhum thum (kangaroo) – then Thomson shoot it.
Sometime we would just be walking and the dog smell it and run
after it. We give some to him too. I think it was a her, a female.

Sometimes my father find the swollen tree, we call that tree "munḏaka".
He said, "This is gapu here" and we got water from the swollen tree,
also we got the gum out of that tree, not only that – he also tell me
how to treat the bark, how to chew, how to get the more satisfaction.
And then firstly when you take it off, it is very difficult – that's the
same bark we make string, bush string.

*The swollen trunk of the munḏaka tree
can be drained for water.*

    And then we find special water for dry season,
    he have to tell me where to dig the hole for gapu
    or if not we have to follow the birds.
    The birds can lead you to where the gapu is, the
        special place.
    They know where the waterhole is,
    You see, smell and flower and he has been follow them.

And Dr Thomson used to say, "Why you done that?" And he used to
say, "To get water" and we used to go and dig and explain.

    There is a muddy Ŋaymil name of place.
    Huge River, which is very muddy, very dangerous crocodile
    and shark live on river too, but one of the Ŋaymil man
        (owner of the land) was with us,
    he put the sweat from under his arms, clapped his hands and
        hit the water
    and spread it saying "shhht, shhht",
    so nothing will come to harm us,
    and then he talk the special language.
    And then we make a wooden raft

and we put that Balanda Donald Thomson on the raft and
    we went across to the other side
and we are also crawling in mud, mud is right up to
    your knees.
We were still on Ŋaymil area, round about 100 mile to
    Warramiri land and then to Dholtji, this is my mother
    place and you can go wherever you please.
This area belongs to my mother.

We are not far from the place where we are to meet boat and
Galarrwuy's father. They waiting for us there, maybe two days later.
They are waiting – Maṯa-Maṯa near English Company Islands,
Warramiri country. We arrive there. Thomson was thankful to my
father, because he arrived there safely.

After that then we leave Thomson and everyone and we go around
and get the canoe. We went back past Elcho Island and then straight
through to mother's place, which is the Wessel Islands, and I meet
some people there. The Wessel Islands belong to my mother's brothers and her uncle. My father took me there, and also my mother's
brother, my uncle, taught me about the totem.

My uncle (my mother's brother) he show my father the
    design of the Warramiri
and sacred objects of the Warramiri
and my uncle said to my father,
"You take this one, learn, and I will show you because you
    have the boy,
Warramiri son, teach him design." and that is how I have
    two designs I can paint.

That was a great thing in my life, then we come back to Yirrkala.
Then he stay there and then took me right round again to Yalaŋbara,
also he took me as far as Trial Bay, and he taught me the different area
which is Gumatj area, Djapu area, Gälpu area, which is one land, but
it's divided but no one ever realised it. It is very difficult for people to
understand but I been go through that and that is why I am able to
think more clearly, not only the painting but the story and land. Now
I start to teach. I trying with the spear out through the bush show
them to see the kangaroo, how to track the kangaroo, just as I learnt
and tell them, "This is the red kangaroo footprint, this is the other
footprint, this is the emu footprint, this is the kookaburra footprint,
you can notice this is the footprint, you can recognise them, not only
the name, but also eat, cooking, how to track them, where to find
them, where is good place to hunt." Also I am teaching my son how
to find the turtle, the turtle under the water. I used to be teaching him
by the lippa-lippa (canoe) but now I taught him instead on the boat.

Donald Thomson

And I am standing beside him,
just like at night too my father used to come and then it was
     nice and calm
and you could see the phosphorescence
and you could see the fish there in the night.

You have to quietly fish, see very carefully,
see where the turtle is in the night, or the dugong,
you have to be careful.

One day I will teach you.
There is many thing on the land learning from my father.
This is my story,
and this is my life story,
and there will be more a bit later on, if you come again.

*Wandjuk Marika spear fishing at
Yalaŋbara – "You have to fish quietly,
see very carefully."*

PLANE CRASH ON BREMER ISLAND – AMERICAN OR JAPANESE?

NOTES

This account of finding the American pilot on Dhambaliya, Bremer Island, recalls the same incident as that recounted by Wandjuk in Gumatj language, published by Yirrkala Literature Production Centre and illustrated by his eldest son Mawalan. Flt Lt Clarence Sandford had apparently taken off from somewhere in the Pacific with other American planes in pursuit of Japanese bombers. When his radio was destroyed he found he was lost and out of fuel so he parachuted into the sea just off Bremer Island. After cutting himself free of his parachute, he swam to shore where he collapsed. He was later transferred from Yirrkala to Darwin on the Mission boat *Larrpan*. On March 28, 1942, he stayed with Ella Shepherdson, wife of the Elcho Island missionary "Sheppy" (Reverend Shepherdson). Ella had taken refuge at Wuraḻŋura due to potential bombing activity. Sandford was transferred to Milingimbi and thence Darwin, after which no further word or information about him could be obtained, although military historians in Darwin have attempted to do so. The survival of Flt Lt Sandford was entirely due to Wandjuk and his relatives. He was very lucky, as during those years people only visited Bremer once a week by dugout canoe.

When I was about 19 years of age, when the holidays had come, I was going out across the sea with three friends, to Bremer Island, Dhambaliya. That was the time we were learning about the war, in school, about the planes and Japanese. We didn't have any sail, so we were paddling to get across there in our canoe, and it was hard, paddling was very hard because the seas were rough and it was getting very dark. We followed the evening star, djurrpuṉ…it showed us the way to that island.

> On the way I caught some turtle with my fish spear
> so we landed on that island at midnight.
> Then, we cooked that turtle.
> We heated the stones, put them inside his neck
> and cooked the meat.
> Then we cut it in pieces to eat.

We stayed overnight there and in the morning we separated – one to the eastern side of that island and two of us, me and Roy's eldest brother, we went to the western side to collect turtle eggs and go fishing. We caught enough fish and got the eggs and it was midday. We were hungry, we want our ŋatha (food) so we make a fire with firewood and make the firesticks. But then, suddenly, as soon as we make the firestick, we heard one of the planes, probably coming from New Guinea. We learn about these planes in school – Japan red circle, British blue and white, and America stars. We were all taught to look for the planes.

That pilot tried to find Australia, or Australian airstrip to land it, but we got no airstrip in those days. Only we have airstrip in Milingimbi. Roy's brother said, "Look, look, look, something coming up," and I said, "Well, that's not a plane, maybe it's the wind. Yes, it's the wind, because it was very windy day. Yes, that's the wind, see the whistling tree, it's bending over," and then he said, "No, no, no, I can see the plane in the air coming across the sky." "Oh yes," I said, then I left everything – fish, fire, and turtle eggs.

When we looked up again a second time we saw the man jump out by parachute and then Roy's brother held my hand tightly and dragged me into the bush. But I said, "No, no, that's the Balanda (white man) jumped from the plane by parachute, we go to look and try to find him." And then we ran across through the bush to try to find this man and see whether he is alive or whether he is dead.

We went to another part of the island, a very long way across the bush, a very long way across the bush, to the other side, east side, of the island. As we were looking at the sea, that place was all calm, blue sea water. Roy's brother said, "What that one there?" I looked and then I knew, "That's the plane now, crash on the sea." I said to him, "We have to keep walking along this beach and see if we can find somebody, whether he alive or whether he dead." And then we walk along the beach until we find this man lying on the beach, on the edge of the water. He only have a singlet and shorts.

Above: *Daily life along the Yirrkala creek in 1959. Yirrinyina is seated in the foreground.*

Below: *Many islands off the coast of Yirrkala were visited occasionally by Yolŋu to hunt.*

65

Above: *Children in a dug-out canoe at Yirrkala in 1959. Wandjuk paddled a similar lippa-lippa to Dhambaliya when the plane crashed.*

Below: *Stone fish-trap near Raɲi, 1959.*

He had nothing anything. He was barefoot. He was lying down there and then I tried to take off my school trousers to try to swim across to the little island, Rooky Island. Then that man was get up and look up and saw us standing round the point, Sandy Point. He was get up and he start to salute, and, OK, we saw he was a man.

At the same time he started to walk along the beach towards us. We were frightened, and Roy's brother he grabbed me again and dragged me into the bush, but I said, "No, no, no, let me alone, we will have to see who is it, the man, maybe he's a Japanese." Then we walk towards him and he walk towards us. He salute, we salute, because I learn it in school about saluting.

> Then we walked face to face,
> he walking towards us and we walking towards him.
> I get ready to spear him,
> holding the fish spear above my shoulder, ready,
> and then I said to him, "Stop right there",
> and he stopped right there.

And then I asked him, "Hey, can you tell us who you is? Australian or British or somebody else?" And he answer us right back, "I am Japanese." So! I was ready to spear him with my fish spear, then he said, "No, no, no, no, I am an American."

> Otherwise I would have killed him with my spear,
> and then he would not have been able to talk.

Then I said, "OK, come towards me." And then he said, "I lose my plane. It drown right on the sea and I just been swim, maybe one mile or two." He was very lucky he landed on the shore safely, otherwise he would have died right there in the middle of the sea.

> OK,
> then I grab him and take him to camp where I was staying
> and feed him fish and turtle eggs.

> Later on he was holding me in the night.
> He was holding me very tight,
> because he is scared of those two brothers.
> He thought they might kill him.

I told him, "Don't you worry, we're going to sleep right here. Tomorrow I am going to take you home to Yirrkala mission, and then we will feed you, because you are one of our friends, an American, or Yankee man or whatever you're called."

When we wake in the morning I cooked the rice for him and tea and sugar. We all ate rice – but we were thinking of the turtle eggs we left behind.

> We settle down
> and then the big wind came up.

66

The waves grew higher, the current came up,
it was very strong wind.
We try to calm the water down by singing
and we did, it was calm again.
Then we put him on the canoe but we leave most of the turtle eggs behind. We only took some of them. Then we start to paddle across back to Wirrawa where the township Nhulunbuy is now.

We came to the beach but there was no one there. Now it is called Gove, today you call it Gove. We paddled across landing on the other side, the mainland, and then he asked us, "Where is the mission?" and then I told him, "Nobody lives in this area, mission is about 15 miles away, we're going to walk along the beach."

The wrecks of World War II planes have been gathered into a display at Gove Airport.

The American was very sick, very tired and very sunburnt. He had nothing to wear, barefoot. We take him right up through towards Yirrkala, but it took long time, and **he** was thirsty, **we** were thirsty. It was a hot day, probably near November.
All the fresh water gone, nothing left,
dry up, dry season.
We walk along, on and on,
and all of a sudden his feet was burning
because the sand is hot, very hot.
I used to it wearing nothing, just barefoot.
We walked towards Yirrkala.
Then we came to the small waterhole, we give him the last water, fill up the dripping bottle.

Half way there, at Mount Dundas, or Djawulpa, I sent one of Roy's brothers to go and get shoes for him and also water and food because by this time he was very sick. I thought we were going to keep on going but he said to me, "OK, Wandjuk – I'm so tired. You tricked me, you're going to take me to the Japanese camp."

And I said, "No, no, no, we're not going to take you to the Japanese camp, we're taking you to the mission. We have just been on school holidays, and now I'm going to take you there so that the missionaries can look after you."

And he said to me, "I won't believe you." Sounds like he called me a "black bastard". But I didn't take any notice of what he was saying because he was so tired.

All his face, shoulder, feet were very burnt. I said "OK, I'm still going to take you. It doesn't matter if you are saying bad words, swearing at me, I'll still take you along home to the mission." And he kept sitting, walking and sleeping maybe another three miles.

Raiding turtle nests for their delicious eggs.

Then, there was the sign,
the sign of the cross
right on the top there at Yirrkala point.
I said "OK, if you don't believe me,
we are going to climb that point, up that hill
and we're going to see the sign of that cross,
like this one here you have
around your neck
on your chest made of silver.
That Jesus was crucified on the cross.
Here is the cross here
and that is the cross there of the mission."
And he saw it.

We got further along the beach, we found Yirrkala and we saw all the Yolŋu running towards us from the mission, carrying tomahawks, spear, nulla nulla (club), all sorts of things. They thought we found a Japanese, but I told them "No" and we kept walking and walking and walking to mission to meet big mob carrying spear and tomahawk, nulla nulla, men and women, girls and boys, run after him – and the American was scared of them and grabbed me but I said to him, "No, no, just relax, these are the missionaries, they bring the food and tools."

They meet us half way on the beach and we gave him food
    and water
and then he was grateful and shake hands
and said, "Thank you."
And then we took him to the old mission house
and everybody is rushing saying,
"Where is he come from?"
"What is he?"
"What kind of Balanda is this?"
"What kind of a colour is this?"
"What kind of face is this?"
And I said to these people,
"Relax, you don't know what you are talking about!"

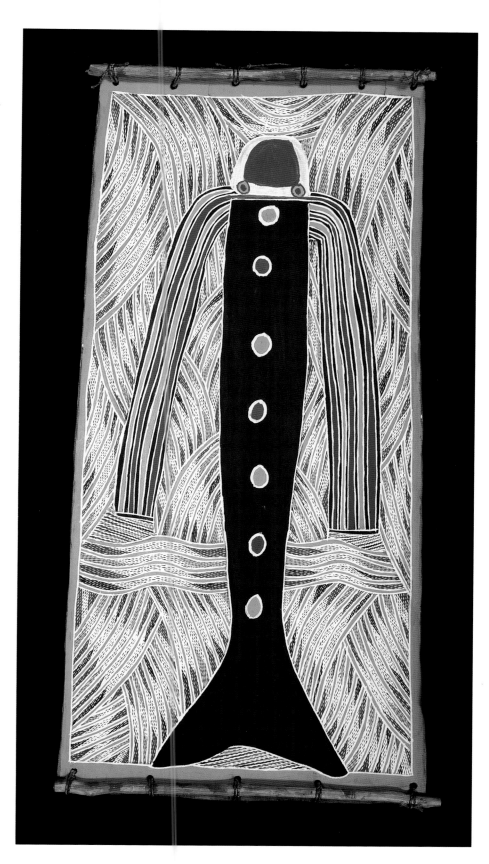

Bark painting by Wandjuk Marika, 1982.

"Daymirri, the sea creature, half whale with long whiskers, that lives in the sea off Dhambaliya." – Rärriwuy Marika

NOTES

In this chapter, Wandjuk's reminiscences of different events and circumstances are interwoven in his memory – the building of the airstrip at Gove in 1940, the coming of the Royal Australian Air Force during the War and the exploration for minerals. Shortly after helping to build the airstrip, he left to hunt crocodiles to earn money from the sale of their skins.

After Japan entered the War, the ratio of Europeans to Aborigines changed drastically in the Northern Territory and the area around Yirrkala was no exception. A major Royal Australian Air Force base was developed at Melville Bay and over 500 servicemen lived only seven kilometres away from the Yolŋu community gathered at the Mission. These "ordinary" Australian men of RAAF squadron No. 13 were different from missionaries, trepangers or government visitors, the Yirrkala

Yolŋu people's only outside Balanda contacts until this time. A camaraderie developed and friendships were made.

Throughout the War years, the Missions acted as agents for the armed forces in managing and organising Aboriginal participation. Local Yolŋu did all the hard physical labour for constructing airstrips with axes, picks and shovels. Trees had to be cleared and grubbed out from many acres. Missionaries were also nominally the coastwatchers although Yolŋu did the actual observing and reporting (see previous chapter), and the missionaries then simply passed on this information. Despite this cooperation between the missionaries and the armed forces, the Missions frequently complained of the familiarity which developed between air force personnel and "natives".

Defence preparation at Darwin increased with the coming of the War. By May 1941, the RAAF had arranged the construction of airstrips at remote Aboriginal missions on the flanks of Darwin, but the army became concerned that the strips could be seized by the Japanese and used as bases for an attack on Darwin. They were isolated and virtually undefended.[8]

As a result of this the army commenced its enlistment of Aborigines as coastwatchers and Wandjuk also began to hunt crocodiles for money.

---

8   Robert A. Hall, *The Black Diggers*, Allen & Unwin, North Sydney, 1989, p. 86.

WAR TIME, BAUXITE AND CROCODILES

After I sent that man back to Darwin, he must have spread the story to the people, the army or air force or navy. A long time after that, later, maybe around about 1943, a boat arrived at Yirrkala. It was still during the War. The Balanda tried to find a man like me or somebody else to guide them and show them about the place. They were looking for a good place, flat country or gravel, so they could make an airstrip. I did that work because I was the only one who spoke English to translate to show them. I was ask my daddy, my father. I said to my father, "Should I to show them my place?" And he said, "Yes". So the air force men took me and we landed in Melville Bay, which is now the big mining site.

Carting timber back to the mission, 1959.

> Maybe they were really looking in two ways,
> for bauxite
> and also an airstrip,
> but I didn't know much about it in those days.

They took me around and I showed them a good place, flat country of gravel. It took us about six weeks to go through there. I got very slim, skinny, because there was a very sharp grass there, but today you hardly see any grass at all. Today there is a straight road, a bitumen road and the concrete line where they load on the bauxite. Anyway, I guided them and showed them a good place. I didn't know there was bauxite there. Yes, maybe, at the same time they were looking to make airstrip. They dug a hole to test the ground – for the bauxite. Because it was gravel road that we had there. I was the man to find that place, and also there was one of my tribal brothers. That place is Gove Airport today and now we have the huge bauxite mine.

The air force men came and set up a camp near that airstrip.
> And then we,
> Yolŋu,
> working there during the War.

Opposite: After clearing the airstrip during the war, Yolŋu laboured at the mission – here they help missionary Douglas Tuffin with the vegetable crop, 1959.

Then after that end of the War they leave everything, nothing left, they take all the equipment back to home. At the same time they want me to go with them to Sydney to work more, but my father said "No, I want my son to be stay on so that I can teach him. I only have one son, no one except him to teach the Law."

Yes, well, soon the War was finished, stopped. It was round about 1945 and I had no more work with Balanda.

The Yolŋu were clearing the airstrip. These men should be old people now but they are all gone,
>they are dead,
>nobody is alive today.
>Only one old man who worked on the airstrip
>and he is very weak,
>maybe he is going to finish or get sick or pass away soon.
>He is getting old and weak
>and his hand is shaking.
>He's mad now in the head.

Not long after, maybe 1950, there was another mob coming up, BHP.[9] We didn't know what they been looking for. They were digging all the places to get the ground underneath. But nobody ever told us what they were looking for. All the old people were helping and I was with them. I was sort of the leading man because I knew how to operate about the Balanda and talk to them. We were drilling their hole for them and it was very hard, sometimes my hand was getting blistered. There was not any machinery in those days, just drilling with the hand to get to the sand underneath.
>Nobody *ever* tell us what they were looking for.
>And then they are gone,
>gone back home.
>We didn't know what to do,
>have **no idea,**
>we **have no idea.**
>No one explained about that work.
>…Too late now.

Then we were on our own. Missionaries were still there, but it was hard to find the rupiah. We didn't have any rupiah, any money, only little money, maybe $20 or $15 or $6 or $8. I don't know why we need the money in those days. Probably we need a boat. Those days it was very hard to get a boat or car or whatever. But today it is different – everything changing.

---

9   The Broken Hill Proprietary Company Limited – Australian mining company.

I used to work to collect trepangs, or sea slugs. I was working and working, thinking how to raise the rupiah. We had a lot of people coming up to Australia to look for trepang, from Indonesia, Singapore – Chinese places. And so we tried to get them ourselves and sell them to the mission.

> We would just dive into the water –
> you can see them everywhere,
> then fill up the canoe.
> Then we dragged the canoe to the beach,
> cut them up there, and clean it out like fish.
> Then we made a bit of a shelter there
> with wire on top.
> Then we put rows of trepang on top
> and underneath it a fire to dry it out.
> There are so many at Yalaŋbara.
> I don't eat them
> but I think they are manymak tucker,
> like bailer shell.
> Then we had to stop getting trepang.
> Everything stopped.

We always worry for rupiah then, always worry. So we have to just sit down, make spear. I don't know why we needed the money – probably for a boat, to go fishing. Those days it was very hard to get a boat or car – but this day it is different, changing everything.

Round about this time when we worrying for rupiah, the missionary tell us about the newspaper and read it to us. They wanted people to get crocodile skins. They said to us, especially my father and all my family, "OK, boys, go and get the crocodile skins." The missionary talk to my father especially because he know how to hunt – to sneak for the crocodile. So that was how we started working on crocodile hides around Melville Bay. We would pick up a canoe and go out during the night with the torch. We always caught some, maybe two or three, four in one night. We were working on crocodile hides for about two years round in Melville Bay. We sent them to Darwin and then they sent our money back.

> Sometimes we use to walk, me and my father,
> across the bush to other side of Arnhem Bay
> to collect more crocodile hide,
> because during the rain, and at night,
> the crocodiles came up from the sea to lay their eggs.
> It was a good time for us to hunt during the wet season time,
> we could get crocodiles easier.
> We use to walk from Arnhem Bay to Yirrkala once a week,
> no car,
> no nothing.

We walked back and sold the hides to the missionary, get money, get

flour, tea and sugar and carry back to the bush to the other side of Arnhem Bay. We were living there for a year, maybe 12 months.

> I was always walking back through the bush
> and that is why I know more about the land,
> more about the story,
> where to go through,
> what to find on the way to Arnhem Bay.

I walk one whole day to Yirrkala and sell the hides, next day Arnhem Bay to get more crocodile.

Every two or three days we were skinning the crocodile hides and taking them back to the mission. Otherwise, after a day, it would stink rotten or smell bad and then we used to stay at Arnhem Bay for four days or six days before take the hides back to the mission. We used to carry the flour on our shoulder, tea and sugar, everything small. Not the smoke like we have today, cigarettes and tin tobacco, we used to have stick tobacco, black stick tobacco – Balanda sell it to us after the War.

> All of a sudden somebody have been passed away who
>   belonged to that area, belong to Arnhem Bay area,
> one of the Djapu clan,
> father of Daymbalipu, he was got drowned in the sea
> in the lippa-lippa (dug-out canoe)
> because of the crocodile
> and then they said to my father,
> "Look, Mawalan, we have to stop hunting and collecting the
>   crocodile hide there because one of the men,
> the owner of Arnhem Bay,
> is passed away.
> We don't want you to go there – maybe some other time."
> And then we stop and start to do our own works
> which is painting.

TRANSLATING THE CHRISTIAN BIBLE

The missionary who is my first teacher is Mr Chaseling and his wife. Because I want to learn more about the other life, Balanda world, they teaching how to read and write.

> At first my uncle he taught me
> nothing any pen and paper. I used rocks,
> and then I learn how to write on the rocks,
> my book was the sand and the leaves and the piece of tree,
> the coconut was the start of writing.

I try to draw fish, animal, turtle, crocodile or animals – and crocodile track with my foot. Also Mrs Thornhill taught me longhand writing – "OK, boys, no worries" – in the mission house (underneath the cliff at Yirrkala). I knew already from my uncle on Elcho Island, he teaching me writing English word. And then she said to me, "I put you in the first class." So she did. And maybe two or three years later, she put me as a teacher assistant.

Beulah Lowe came and not long, when we start to translate from the Bible. They start me on translate into Gumatj language. The Old Testament translating from there to New Testament, not only that, but, at the same time, the hymn book, used to be called the Methodist Hymn Book. I remember some of those.

> Yes, there's David,
> David make the song like the angel,
> and the Lord
> and the birthday of Jesus, journey to Nazareth,
> and that sort of thing and many others.

OK. I was start to learn the Balanda way, see the way learning and working. Not only that but at the same time while I was been teaching, I translate from the Old Testament and New Testament to Yolŋu language. We use that today – Gumatj and Gupapuyŋu – same pronunciation. Teaching them, working with Beulah Lowe, to translating the Old and New Bible.

NOTES

The first missionary in Yirrkala was Wilbur Chaseling who is remembered for teaching reading. Wandjuk records that another missionary, Mrs Thornhill, taught him to write, although he had already learnt to make the alphabet from his mother's brother, a Warramiri clan leader from Elcho Island. The Warramiri people, his mother's clan, continued to teach, nurture, protect and look after him throughout his life even in the face of death. The theme of the protective powers of warramiri (the octopus) recurs frequently in Wandjuk's life story.

As is clear from the text, Wandjuk perceived many Judaeo-Christian values to be the same as those of Yolŋu but he felt that Yolŋu culture had already contained the basic precepts of Christian teaching…well before the Christians found out about them.

Bark painting by Mawalan Marika, c. 1957.

The Reef of Ŋulwaḏuk with its Sea Animals.

This painting depicts the Reef of Ŋulwaḏuk with its totemic creatures. Ŋulwaḏuk was the Ancestor figure associated with the sea bed and coral reef. He was the progenitor of Marryalyun, the ancestral figure of the sea. The crayfish is the totem of the Warramiri. At the bottom are shellback turtles, guwarrtji. The arcs on each side of the turtles are the sacred rocks. Above the turtles on the right is a squid.

One fits into our story similar to our story,
like honour thy mother and father, that sort of thing.
Do not commit adultery.
It is the same thing in our word
which is, do not steal – yaka manaŋi,
yaka buma – which is do not kill,
and yaka manaŋi – honour thy mother and father,
honour your sister, rely on your sister,
not allowed to talk to your sister or whatever.
This is our law,
the Christian before the missionary world, and it is from
    my father's father,
or more from before my father's grandfather.
They said we should carry on like them.
Djaŋkawu and Wawilak is our law,
similar to missionary laws.

When you very unhappy if someone murdering your relative
    or your very close friend
and you sad for many weeks,
then you start to make yourself happy,
you bring whoever is against your law, take him into the
    Djaŋkawu and Wawilak law ceremony.
So you can teach him to become aware of the law.
Our own word before missionaries have land, is to **teach**
never be unkind to anyone.
My father Mawalan always tell me,
"Yes. There is the Balanda coming.
I don't know whether manymak Balanda or yätj Balanda.
Missionaries is OK, but there is bad people."
We knew what was happening in his life
because he was see all this from when I was born,
because he was going with other people.
He knew Macassan people.
That's why he knew the painting
because my grandfather, Märi, has told him,
but he see what kind of a marks, material
and he seen the other things.

He taught me all that sort of thing, and then when the missionaries come, wanting to hear history of the law, our culture and Mawalan said, told what he knew and he said "I'm not going to be Christian but I come as a Christian to the missionary to learn about the Bible, because your story fit into our story, but my story is Law and is Christian before you arrive."

I think we come to the church, but we not Christian.
I pretending to be Christian, but I not Christian.

Above: *Children lined up for school, 1959.*

"In our school now I teach very differently – it's not assimilation any more. We teach in our own language and use our own script as we have in this, my father's story."
    – Rärriwuy Marika, 1995.

Below: *Exuberant children in front of the camera outside the mission store, 1959.*

My father he teach me because he knew what was going
    to happen,
because we **live** the story that Balanda had been **teaching**.

And some other anthropologist told my father, "The missionary life is
short but yours is long, keep your life and culture." That's what Dr
Warner told us, the first anthropologist to visit Yirrkala. And then

*Bark painting of Djaŋkawu and his two
mawalan – sacred walking sticks, done by
Wandjuk Marika during the Land Rights
case, 1972.*

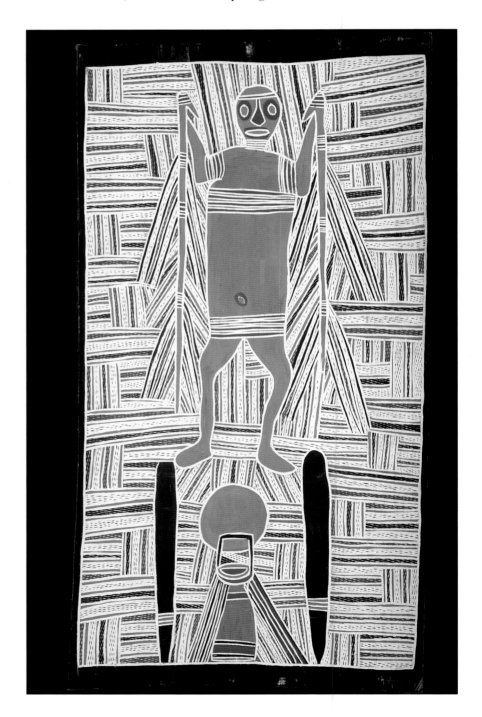

after I became more understanding I try all the writing, teaching about the Bible, also the hymn book, also translating for another anthropologist Professor Berndt.

Yes. When I was teaching, start to teach in the Balanda world. Then I realise how Balanda operate. How it began here, but I was only heard roughly from Balanda, which is first settlers arrived in Australia, other part of Australia, like Melbourne and Sydney, Botany Bay, and then they settle down and establish a city, big city to live in. Then after that, I know different part of Australia learning not only the teaching way, but also the experience.

> At the same time, my mind grow
> both sides.
> First, have a knowledge and experience of my own world
> before I become as a teacher's assistant.
> Second, Balanda.

I was been teaching for four-and-a-half years, then I was get sick. At the same time when I was teaching the big fighting was still on. Yolŋu fighting, Yolŋu war, fighting each other, tribe to tribe. Before Balanda collected all the Yolŋu together at Yirrkala, we been travelling around fighting, Yolŋu to Yolŋu. And also I learn about the Christian how to forget the anger, how to control the people, how to stop the Yolŋu fight.

> I am friendly, I am kindly each other,
> not hatred each other, have to bring them as a one group.
> Not only that, but there is a Balanda way **cooperate**.

But there is another law, like märrma (two) law – the two Yolŋu laws is Djaŋkawu and Wawilak ceremony, and all that ceremony before the missionary. Because the missionary tell us how to do good behaviour.

> There is two – Djaŋkawu and Wawilak
> the first Christians, the first peacemakers.
> I'm telling you this
> that Djaŋkawu and Wawilak was the first Christians to
>   make peace and make the friendship.
> No matter whoever got killed,
> who take miyalk from the other tribe.
> Djaŋkawu and Wawilak made peace.
> My people, my father's grandfather and my grandfather used
>   to have peace,
> my father's ceremony was for friendship.

Notes

After extreme conflict, if someone has been murdered, or if there is a serious resolution to be achieved, this can be accomplished by inviting the enemy to participate in Djaŋkawu and Wawilak ceremonies.

Wandjuk's behaviour throughout his life in the Balanda world was primarily designed to bring Balanda close to Yolŋu, to teach them about Djaŋkawu and Wawilak. His speeches, thinking and talking were consistent with this philosophy.

This chapter also briefly recounts his contact with some of the most impor-tant anthropological writers of the early twentieth century. His father Mawalan worked with W.L Warner, author of A *Black Civilization*, and also Professor A.P. Elkin of Sydney University. When Wandjuk was about 18, Professor R.M. Berndt and his wife Catherine spent a considerable time working with the community with Mawalan and Wandjuk. A great many papers, articles and books resulted from this contact, leaving Wandjuk in later life, whenever he observed the books, to comment, "If he is professor then I am Vice Chancellor…but nobody give me salary." Wandjuk also felt he was due acknowledgement and payment for the use of his "knowledge" (or intellectual property) contained in anthropological writings such as the Berndts'.

In emphasising the role of Djaŋkawu and Wawilak, Wandjuk also refers to a period of social and religious upheaval on Elcho Island in the 1970s. The clan leaders became split over a fundamen-talist Christian movement developing on Elcho Island. An incident occurred in which some of the most sacred ritu-al objects, usually kept in hiding, were put on display. Mawalan's teaching meant Wandjuk could never agree to or condone this.

ELCHO

I have the painting and story written on a calendar, you probably know the calendar. That the story I was just do out from school, and then we had a big meeting, a big meeting, in Elcho Island – the Warramiri people, my mother's people.

This is about how the mission try to change and the first of the missionaries (Rev. Shepherdson but he's still alive), he said to the gathering of all the old people,

> Gathering all the old people and he said to them,
> "Look, OK, old people we need you to bring all the things,
>   all your sacred dilly bag, sacred objects and whatever you
>   have.
> Make the big fire and burnt offering,
> burn all your culture."

Do you know what happened at Elcho Island when all the sacred objects were made public? My father was very disappointed and told very strong words and to everybody to every tribe, from Yirrkala to Elcho.

> He said, "Stop doing all this thing.
> Don't ever show sacred objects to this missionary or to the
>   public.
> Now if you're going to show this, how are your children
>   going to keep their sacred laws?
> How are they going to keep themselves strong?
> When the Balanda come, the Balanda going to ask them,
>   'Where's the culture?'
> and the children are going to say they got no culture. That
>   means **you** got no respect for **your** young ones. You must
>   look after and teach your children."

No, I'm not going to show my sacred objects.
I'm going to keep my sacred objects,
going to teach my son so he can teach his children.

Opposite: *Although sacred emblems and feathered objects have been revealed to the public in other communities, Wandjuk's father Mawalan urged his own family to keep these only for special ceremonies. The feathered strings made from the feathers of lindirritj (rainbow lorikeet) are used in most ceremonies.*

81

> You don't know, one day Balanda going to come and ask my
> 　　child, my boy,
> and what is he going to say to him?
> If he is going to say he got no culture, what Balanda going
> 　　to say?
> He gonna kick him out, take all his land.
> My father, he said, "Bring your culture back."
> My children and every clan, learnt more about what they
> 　　had lost.
> And today they've got it, their children have got it,
> the land, the culture.

And then some other people, my tribe or my family or another group of people, they been destroy and threw everything away and become a Christian – still some of them are Christian. But they always come and ask *me* exactly the same as they used to ask my father to *show* them, to *guide* them and to hold the culture so that *they* can hold their culture, and law and ceremony.

And then they went to Elcho and they setting up the big meeting there and they make all the things, all the sacred objects to display and put it for the public (to see).

> And my father was there and he said to me,
> "I am going to talk to them,
> OK, what the news?"
> he asked them, "What the news?"
> and he said, "I'm keeping the Law, I'm not going to destroy
> 　　because I have a son to teach the mother story,
> the painting and sacred ceremony and sacred object – all my
> 　　own ceremony,
> always grandma ceremony, märi ceremony,
> or maḏayin sacred object
> and buŋul, dance.

Yes this was very long and difficult for me. I was been working in our own culture and own law learning from eight years of age until my father passed away till now. I have all experience in my mind and knowledge to carry on to my children, to learn and teach them many things, painting and singing and show them the movements, so that they can carry on what I have been done in the past and carry to their children what I have passed to them.

LOVE MAGIC

About the time when I was teaching, working as the teaching assistant at the school in Yirrkala, some big trouble was coming up. One of the Djambarrpuyŋu men thought that I was fighting with the other people, the other group, Gälpu. One of the men's wives was my girlfriend, they thought that I was fighting against them, but I wasn't. I try to help these people to stop hurting each other.

Suddenly one man picked up a big stick,
quite a big stick with a sharp point –
he threw it at me;
hit my chest right here.
Good job Flying Doctor was there.
And when he hit me, I fell down on the ground,
blood is shooting up just like a big lump, like a boil.
You could hear blood coming up nearly bust up
and I try to get the stick and break it off
but the doctor say, "No, No."
He give me an injection, and the lump was going down,
    otherwise I would have been finished.

Then the Flying Doctor took me to Darwin Hospital,
and I was there for three weeks
and that's where I lost my nerves in my hand.
That's why I have a funny hand, on my left hand,
because doctor said the nerves had collapsed.
When I play yidaki (didjeridu) I can hear it [my chest]
    rushing and I stop.
When I am driving also I feel stiff.
But anyhow,
I went to Darwin Hospital for 3 weeks
and then I get better and I walk round there.
I was relaxed.
Then somebody came up to me.
I forget his name,

NOTES

Wandjuk's knowledge of love songs and his interest in the strengths of love "magic" or sorcery was well known. For Wandjuk the power of sexual attraction was often expressed in dreams as well as in life, and he believed the person dreamt of shared the experience.

The youthful saga of love magic he describes here reveals the strength of women's magic, particularly mysterious women from faraway places. To recover he needed marrŋgitj medicine, the power of his Warramiri kin *en masse*, his mother's heart and finally the perpetrators themselves to reverse the sorcery.

Wandjuk's input into Ronald Berndt's book *Love Songs from Arnhem Land* was extensive. He occasionally showed amusement at the dutiful recording of all a young boy's sexual ideas – he thought he was helping out an old Balanda who knew nothing about sex and wanted ideas and advice!

83

to take me for advice on arts and crafts in Northern
    Territory,
to be travelling from Darwin to Port Keats and collect all
    the paintings.
Now this story make me to think of those two miyalk
    (women) of Port Keats.

This is about the miyalk
the powerful women of Port Keats.
Märrma (two) miyalk sing love songs,
strong ones and dangerous ones.
We drove to the camp at Port Keats to buy the art for
    Welfare Branch.
I was staying in the single quarters.
I don't know how to play around with the women because
    my mind was not clear.
I wanted to learn more about the Balanda world.
Then all of a sudden these two miyalk jumped me,
they passed me,
teasing me to play around,
because those days I was a very handsome man, slim,
today I am a fat man.
I said, "No", and those miyalk said, "Yo"
and I say, "Why?"
they said, "Come with us, you will find out about us" –
I did!

I don't know then what they would do.
We were driving back to Darwin, the Welfare Branch man
    and myself,
then half way on the plain country these two girls,
are still in my mind,
and I was saying, "Go away, go away
because I'm on Balanda work now."
And then we were in the plains country
and I saw those girls, walking in the plain country, near
    an ant hill.
I saw those two girls coming up toward us
and I said to driver, welfare man or whatever,
I said, "Look that's the two girls that coming up to us."
"You're joking."
"Well, well, you didn't see it – yes, can't you see it?"
He said "I can't see it, I don't know what you talking about",
but they were there.

Those two girls came up to us
and I say "There you are, I can see them now, right now,
    they're walking"

– just like out of the snow, under a mist,
like a shadow coming towards us."
And then we came up to ant hill,
that's the flat one, not the huge one.
And I said, "OK, hold it, they are hiding right here."
We stopped the car and got out.
I said, "Hold it, I'm going to walk around and find them."
But I got there and no one nothing there.

But they got *me*.

When I got out and walked round
there was something, a reflection on my eyes – blue,
   white, red,
like a rainbow, just like a rainbow, right on my eyes.
My eyes just filled up.

The welfare man was looking at me.
He said, "What's wrong with you?"
I didn't say anything.
"I'm going to take you to Darwin Hospital."
He was driving hard, day and night,
because that big river, Daly River, was coming up [rising].
I was still in the car, shaking with emotion,
my body shaking all over.
I stayed overnight in the hospital
and then flew back to Gove.

I thought I was OK so I started working again
and I started painting,
but I still had the same sickness.
And then I was got more sick in head and body,
so I went to see the Yolŋu doctor,
marrŋgitj (sorcerer) man.

Yes, I saw the marrŋgitj
and he drew a round stone from my heart.

Also one of the girls at Yirrkala was making magic –
a marrŋgitj too.
She put sweat all over me
and massaged and squeezed my chest
so the stone and women's hair came out.
The marrŋgitj just walk along
and he saw those two girls behind my back, standing
   very still
and marrŋgitj is coming toward me talking to them.

Wandjuk at Yirrkala, 1959.

85

He called to them,
"OK you two, get out from his back,
we want this man, Wandjuk, to be alive and strong."
And that's how he get rid of those two girls' spirits,
for a while.

But I didn't get better straight away,
so I flew back to Darwin.
All my flesh was gone, I was weak, nothing anywhere,
my bones sticking up, skin hanging.
The doctor was tired and said "We can't do anything,
maybe you will live two to three days."
My eyes were white, I could not recognise anyone.

Then I was in my dream,
I could see a devil monster coming to kill me,
more devil monsters.
That devil is very strong and that bad spirit came towards me
but my relations from Wessel Island come to stop them, stop
    all those devil spirits.
All my relatives came from Wessel Island to get the devil
    monster in a group
what you call, the Octopus or Flying Fox group.
All relatives in a group are strong medicine to fight those
    devil spirits.

I'm well and strong today because I have my mother's heart
    and my own heart.
Two very strong hearts. Yes.
It doesn't matter whoever tries to attack me with the maŋgi
    maŋgi (sorcery),
which is poison arrow pointing at me,
my mother's spirit will always protect me, get rid of them.

When anyone touches me on the neck, I could feel a flash,
a reflection –
that makes me better.
It wasn't a real touch, but it was the spirit of Warramiri,
which is flying fox and octopus.
They had changed to Yolŋu, and came to help me.
With their help I was feel better but I did not think I was
    fully better.

Then one brother of those people,
they really sent him to help me.
He was walk round Darwin because his wife was there.
His wife said, "One of the men from Yirrkala is very sick",

and he said, "OK, don't worry, I'm going to send for
    those sisters
and say 'you have been do bad thing to that man'."

Yes, those two sisters flew to Darwin, went straight
    to hospital.
They went to my room,
the curtain was shut around me and there was a
    notice saying,
"No admittance, three days to go to death."

And those two sisters, they say,
"He is our boyfriend."
So they come in and I see them.
They walked around me.

I didn't know what they would do to me.
They put their sweat all around my forehead,
my face, my body and took their clothes off,
covering me with their bodies.
Then they kissed me.
They were crying for me.
They were sorry that they had done wrong.

I had three days left but it took only one to get better.

Next morning my eyes were open.
I looked around the place and saw just the normal faces,
not strange like when I was sick.
Everything was different in my dream.
There were palm trees everywhere, and beaches surrounding
    the hospital.
I opened my eyes and saw the place.
Then I said to the Sister,
"Hey, Sister, what happened? Where's the palm trees,
    where's the beach?"
"Oh, you thought you were at Yirrkala."
"Yes. Where's the beach, where's the palm trees?"
She said, "What are you talking about?"

Anyway,
then, I just went back to Yirrkala, to make myself strong.
I flew back home, staying there, working.
I was still weak, but at the same time I was strong again.
In Yirrkala I was painting again, until 1953,
with my father.

LOST AT SEA

NOTES

The little aluminium boat that Mawalan bought for Wandjuk in 1963 is still on the beach camp sands at Yirrkala, in the camp known as Raŋi where Wandjuk and his family lived. The story of being lost at sea has assumed legendary status in the young people's minds, a true saga of courage, 12 miles out from shore. When reading this chapter in the manuscript, Wandjuk's eldest son Mawalan recalled that Sheppy, as Rev. Shepherdson was known, received word via radio from the missionaries that Wandjuk was missing. Shepherdson was one of the earliest aviators of the Territory. He owned his own plane which he flew to different settlements in north-east Arnhem Land. After receiving the message he took off from Elcho and landed at Gove where he collected Mawalan, Mawalan II (Wandjuk's eldest son), as well as Wandjuk's younger brother Dhurryurrŋu. The plane took off and Mawalan II recalls that everyone was extremely terrified. It was raining, in the middle of the wet season, and the seas were very high. They flew around Bremer Island until they finally saw the smoke from Wandjuk's fire. Rev. Shepherdson then dropped the food and the note to say that the mission boat would come to collect them the next day.

In 1963 my father bought me boat in Darwin, £863, old rupiah (money). I still have that boat today, in remembrance of my father, he bought me the boat long ago. I was always fishing, I know where to go fishing, my father took me to the spot which is a good fishing area with the dugout. You know he used to make dugout canoe, real thing, that he learnt how to make from his father, my grandfather. He used to take about a week or two weeks to make, and I used to watch him, he make the canoe. He cut the big canoe tree down to make the canoe, and then he taught me fishing in that canoe.

We used to paddling across the sea to Bremer Island – and sometimes I used to take the canoe by myself – paddling across to the island by myself so I can learn what the life is in the sea, what the life on the island is it danger or peaceful. He took me there and show me.

Then the mission come in and everyone try to find aluminium boat – and he bought me one in 1963. One day I just been go fishing, across to Bremer Island, three of us, and it was really a very windy day. I went to one little island, one little island called Yilipaywuy and I was fishing there and collecting the seagull eggs, to collect them and take them back to Yirrkala. And then there was a big wind – I started going back home from that island, that island is Yilipaywuy far across, about 12 mile. Yilipaywuy is island, there, where seagull lay eggs.
    Then I started back,
    starting the motor,
    but the rope was just bust, break, I can't do anything.
    I can't do anything!
    I was just sitting there and I tried to find the bamboo tree
    to split as a paddle
    and I trying hard right up the island.
    I am trying hard, but the wind was very strong,
    very strong, the current was being very strong,
    but the wind was pushed me toward Cape Wilberforce.
    I was just drifting there.
    And my father was been worry.

They thought I was lost, I **was** lost, but I trying hard, try to get back to the island and then I came to the island, which is Rooky Island, called Malirri. The other name of that island is Wuyula which is my little boy's name, name after the island.

But nothing on that island, no water, no nothing – thirsty, because we didn't get any rain in the containers. I thought we would just go back at the same day, but we just get lost on the sea.

The plane was searching for me everywhere, but they couldn't find us, they thought we were just lost forever. We were on the sea for eight days, still drifting around without any water and then the wind changed, take me to the little island, one little island, which is Malirri, near Cape Wilberforce in the middle of the sea – there is a little bit of grass there and some waterhole. I was just paddling and there was this island there and we were thirsty.

Hunting fish with gara (fish spear) and galpu (woomerah).

There were three of us, Wukaka I and his nephew Robert Yunupiŋgu and myself. We landed on that island, we pull the boat right up the beach, not a beach, really, sort of gravel or stone and then I tell them, "Try to find some water." I talk to Wukaka, "Try, some water, see what you can find on that higher up there" and he **did** found that water and we sit there and we had fish there and oysters, but we still wanted to find some food. And one day, next day, I make the bush fire and my brother in Galiwinku, Elcho Island, he was flying trying to look for us 'cause my father was crying, swearing, really worried. He said, "What have you done to my son, try to kill him?"

I was make a bush fire. The first missionary, Rev. Shepherdson or "Djapi" (he was the first missionary), he flew over to look for us, he flew from Elcho in his own plane, and then, all of a suddenly they spotted the bush fire, and they spotted the fire. Then they just circle round and flew back to Yirrkala and picked up ŋatha (food) and then they flew back to drop us some tinned stuff, tea and sugar and some ŋarali (tobacco) on the island and also letters to tell us they would come next day, next morning. Then they did.

They pick us up by boat and my boat was towed back to Yirrkala. I was being on the sea eight days, on the island two days, that's ten days all told, ten days – eight days without the food on the sea – two days on that island before they find us.

> This the story of my life
> many more yet to come when I have a rest and relax,
>   thank you.
> I will tell you more about this writing already,
> but there is many more to come.
> I will tell more about my life story
> and my father's story, which my father has taught me
>   and many more.
> I have to think it over first before we go through again.
> Thank you.

MARRIAGE

When I was 19 years of age, then I get married,
not really get married by love but it was been promised,
my promise wife is not from my own area, Yirrkala.
They promised me in Elcho Island.
The promise is not just from any other tribe, or any
    other languages,
and is not my own close-by relation.

In Yolŋu worlds and Yolŋu law I have to be promised to
    a mother's brother's daughter.
I was married my mother's brother's daughter
we call ŋändi mother,
ŋapipi uncle, the mother's brother.
My mother's brother promised me the daughter for a
    long time
– until I was 19 years of age,
and then they gave her to me – marriage,
and then I was been living with my wife.

After that my mother and my uncle was passed away,
and then, same family, they promised another wife to
    me second.
I should have been married about four in one family,
but I said yaka (no), I only have one or two.

I choose two. The eldest and the very last.
The other sister of my wife is married to someone else.

Then I was been starting to work, like painting
and go through the ceremony, to help other people
and also I been on Balanda's world.
And then, someone else from a different tribe,
    Gumatj tribe,

NOTES

Under Yolŋu traditional law, marriages are negotiated between parents within a set framework of kinship. Dhuwa marries Yirritja and vice versa, and within that certain subgroups are appropriate, or "right way", marriage partners to certain others.

Until recently it was common for two or more sisters to be promised to, and marry, the one man. Marriage was an arrangement often before birth – the young girls went to the camp of their husbands and were eased into married life as they matured. The older wives maintained influence by dint of strength of personality, age, wisdom, status and through their children.

Wandjuk's two wives in Yirrkala, my sisters, first brought me into the family with traditional gifts and exchanges, we remained close always.

Jenny Home (Wulula) and her daughter Mayaṯili (whom Wandjuk called "my princess") now live in Melbourne and share frequent visits from their Yirrkala family. In turn, they visit the family at Yirrkala or Yalaŋbara once or twice a year.

Dhuwandjika preparing stingray for the family: Wuṉarrk, Mawalan, Djaybiny, Giyakmin, their children and grandchildren. Further down the sand Wandjuk is collecting gapu (water).

promised me one girl, as promise wife, to make three,
but that girl –
we have been travelling to Bendigo together to Melbourne
    to opening the exhibition there,
and she was been stay with me for a year
but then when I was been travelling with the Balanda world
    she left me,
fall in love with other man.
Now she is married in Elcho Island.

Yes, then I meet Jenny Home, we meet each other, 1977.
She said to me, "I'm not Aboriginal woman, I'm
    Balanda woman.
I'm a Balanda girl, I don't know anything about it.
Your world is different and my world is different.
I'm not involved in any Yolŋu story, or any Yolŋu lover
    or boyfriend."
But I was said to her,
"Relax, you will learn from me.
I will teach you the Yolŋu way that you don't know,
the name of the land, the birds and the animals,
sea animal and land animal."
I'm teaching her, we had a very hard time.
I was having a very hard time with the family
because I have already two wives and children
and I try to make three wives
and to get away from all this hatred or jealousy.

Yes, jealousy,
not about any women,
but what I know about the sacred law and sacred song from

different part of Arnhem Land,
because they don't know much about the culture,
they know, but they not fully understanding
about the law, how they operate,
but they try to do this before to my father.

Then I take Jenny Home to Yirrkala,
only my sisters and my brothers accepted her.
My two wives doesn't want her to be with me
because she is Balanda and they are Yolŋu.
I'm a Yolŋu married to Balanda, quite a long time,
maybe for three years, and then at last
we found a little Mayaṯili,
because we love each other dear.

*At Minirrki's son's funeral, the senior
family paint the younger members with
sacred Djanda designs. The white clay is
from buwaṯa, bush turkey, and protects the
close kin. From left: Wandjuk Marika,
Napandala, Mayaṯili, Banaminy,
Wayalwaŋa and Rärriwuy.*

Before that my first wife, and second does not love her
   or accepted her,
but also her parent was say something.
"OK Jenny, you not going to marry this man.
He's a tribal man and he's a very important man",
and Jenny is saying to her parent,
"Yes I know, but I love him,
and I'm going to marry him, because he is **the** man.
You got no experience, you got no knowledge."
And then we find the little one, Mayaṯili
through little one, her parent accept me,
and my first wife accepted her, bring her to the family life.
Now we are happy and they are happy.

Every time when the little girl she finished from school,
she always going down to the beach, staying with my
   first wife
and the children – all her brothers and sisters,
she play with them, and that's why she become more
   understanding
about the language,
and that's why Jenny Home is understanding about the
   family system.

When Jenny first come to Yirrkala she was nervous with my first two
wives, she was feel embarrass that I am with her but the other family
– my sisters and Wukaka's family, his wife and his children, Roy's
family, his wife and his children – they accepted me, the whole community accepted her, so we can have a Balanda in our family. If we
have very complicated problem she have to come and help with my
community, my own community. A problem like the Balanda ways,
Balanda sort of coming and asking you and Yolŋu worrying, and she
helps you sort it out, like Roy have a problem, hard to write to get

Wandjuk and his family at Yalaŋbara, 1983.
Left: Mäpupu.
Above: Giyakmin, baby Narripapa and Mäpupu.

Opposite page top: Giyakmin collecting oysters.
Bottom left: Wandjuk wakes with Gomili.
Bottom right: Mawalan and Mäpupu.

Above: *Mayaṯili ready for Buŋgul with her
mothers and brothers in Sydney.
Mayaṯili visits her Yirrkala family often and
participates in ceremonies.*

Below: *At Minirrki's son's funeral,
Wandjuk paints the sacred Djanda designs
on Mayaṯili's body.*

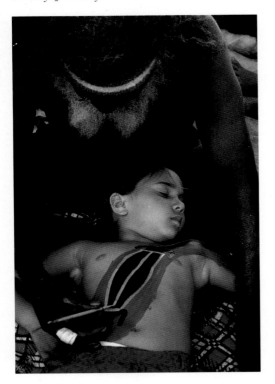

some rupiah, or road or other transport, she try to help Roy's family –
just like Nancy Williams used to do as Roy's secretary, Jenny is doing
that sort of work with the community. Yes, she's working for the community if they need. On the other hand, we want our own organisation, get a grant for our homeland, for Yalaŋbara so we can setting up
our own school or arts and craft shop or whatever.

Because I am travelling in Balanda world, it take me long time to settle down to establish my own place. I have nothing much time to do
my work, because I been travelling a lot on Balanda world. The
Balanda need me to go there, go there, go here and go there. I did
not have time to settle down and think.

In 1982 or 1981, yes 81, I was start to do my painting and make my
exhibition in Sydney. Then I get more money to move out and then I
get all my things preparing, then I move out and settle down now.
Nobody ever help me, even community, even royalty, I did not get
much, no one ever been help me to moving out and staying in my
homeland.

Yirrkala is my spirit landing,
   but most important land is Yalaŋbara,
   which is sacred area and Djaŋkawu's creation land,
   which I have today.
You know why I am not at Yirrkala any more?
Because there is so many rush, rushing, go there, go there,
      go there,
   not talking the Yolŋu way or preparing how we can teach
      the young people,
   they always have a meeting to begging
   or asking for money write the djorra or letter.
We want this, we want that, and that sort of thing.
That why I moving out.
I been thinking for a long time, talking for long time,
   now I'm settled down now.

I'm thinking for something to fill 'er up Yalaŋbara,
   make the water tank or windmill or garden or school
   because Jenny Home going to be a teacher,
   she start to teaching in Yirrkala school,
   to get more Yolŋu feeling, get more understanding
      about Yolŋu,
   but she know already about the Balanda way,
   because she's Balanda,
   but she want to get more understanding,
   because our little girl talking three language already.
Father's language, mother's language and the
      relation language.

96

thought we come from far across the sea, from an Asian country or
Malaysia or India. That meant if we would have been come from that
area, or from Pacific Island, from India or Indonesia or Malaysia, **how**
would we have been know about the land divided up the two moiety,
Yirritja, Dhuwa? How we been know where is very special land?

The Balanda **don't** know, especially the anthropologists or even the
Aboriginal Affairs – they made up all the story. Whoever working
like digging the ground and find the bone that is true, archaeology.
This is true, they prove. But anthropologist, I don't know where they
get their idea from.

> They just study, they study about the Balanda history,
> not the Yolŋu history,
> but they can't understand, they know just a little bit,
> but **outside**, but not **in** it,
> **where** the land is,
> **how** we know each other,
> how we marrying,
> how our creation has been moiety – Yirritja and Dhuwa.

> Our land and also the animals, divided up to two groups,
> also – some animal not allowed for you to kill or eat.
> Some other animal you allowed to eat,
> but not your special totem, like djanda and ḻindirritj.
> These birds always come here and say "Hello" to me and
>   I talk to them.

> The Balanda don't know anything about **what in**
>   the ground.
> They just thought – "oh that's a good country,
> we have to try and find something – mineral, or oil,
>   or copper",
> and they just go and knock the tree
> and knock the rock, the hill,
> make some kind of houses or anything
> because they are careless with the land,
> they want to get something, rich thing, from under
>   the ground.
> They don't care about their land, nothing,
> they don't **know** about the land, and **that** what
>   the **difference**.

We know when we saw the land have been destroy, built the good
houses yes, but spoil the natural ground. Look at it! Today is the big
building, bitumen road, cars, engines, high building – on our mother's earth.

Land that has not changed
  For many a year
Land where my people
  Once dwelt
Its peace has been broken
by the roar of a bulldozer
  Cutting down all the sacred trees
And scarring all the sacred places

  ...And the hearts of my people
    Have broken with it.

Poem written by (Gurramu) Rärriwuy
Marika (age 15) in 1969 during the Land
Rights case.

Above: *Wandjuk making an impassioned speech about land and its religious meaning to Yolŋu. A great yidaki player, he usually played at such occasions. He is holding his own painting of Gomili, a special food plant made by the Djaŋkawu (also his son's name).*

Right: *Wandjuk Marika with the Administrator of the Northern Territory, Commodore Johnson, on the occasion of the award of the Member of the Order of Australia (OAM) to Liyapidiny, at Yirrkala in 1982.*

Now I go back there is big meeting, all the big bosses from Parliament from Canberra coming up and meeting. What they going to do for this land, Yirrkala or Gove or Nhulunbuy. Some world churches come around to Yirrkala, then my name was spread out everywhere round the world. Because I'm been working on many things on Balanda – or with the Balanda.

Then they pick me up again, they pick me at Yirrkala. They take me with them right round Australia, then I beginning to start travelling with the Balanda – not any Yolŋu, nothing, only me – or some of the Yolŋu, not from Yirrkala tribe, but from different part of Australia – travelling around Darwin to Derby, from Derby to Perth by bus. Perth, Western Australia on Christmas Day. We there working and preaching all the gospels about new way of living, then I start working with them. At the same time, my mind was not really involved on the Christian levels. Yes, I can go Christian, but I'm not going to full Christian. I can be Christian but not Christian.

The first petition sent to the Australian Government from the clan leaders in 1963, prior to the first Land Rights case.

And then I've been travelling and I start thinking,
"this is not my life – this is not my culture –
this is not my life – this is not my culture."
Missionary try hard to put me in.
I like to hear their story, the Christian story,
I know that already – that what my feeling was.
Then I travelling right up to Sydney.
We used to staying in Sydney, and then, at the same time,
    some problem was coming.
The mining company, start to clearing the place at
    Nhulunbuy, Gove, Yirrkala, clearing.
But the airstrip was already there.
They tried to teaching me and show me about the
    Christian life.
If I would have been taken deeply in the Christian and if all
    my land been mined
I would have lost my land.
I would have been had nothing.
Law, culture and so on,
and I am happy and I am glad that I have been learn more
    about our own culture first,
before Balanda take me away from my people, travelling
    right round the world.

And then, when we get to Sydney, I was in Sydney with those Christian world churches exchange, and I heard about Jennifer Isaacs. She was been working on Aboriginal Affairs in Sydney as a secretary to Dr Coombs, and then I come and meet her in 1971, and then I talk to her – haven't meet David Isaacs yet, because he was been working as a doctor, and he is a doctor. And I meet her and write her something

about it because I tried to see Dr Coombs, but he was in Melbourne, and I write her a note for Jenny Isaacs to visit me and they said "yes" and she did, she did visit me to Yirrkala and Dr Battersby because they were working in the same office. Mrs Battersby she was with her, Jenny Isaacs, Jennifer, they visit me Yirrkala, and we adopted her as a family and we give her names and kinship.

Then I stay and more work, tried to concentrate what I'm going to do with the land, because no one ever tell us what's going to happening. "There's no land", they said, "you got nothing left. You are only just sitting on top of this land, but you do not own this land" and that was make me more ***think***. Before that time, my father before my father went to hospital, he gave me many things sacred objects and he said, "Show whoever going to come and ask you – maybe they going to help you, maybe they not."

Mawalan Marika, Wandjuk's father, 1947.

In 1969, my first step up in travelling was to Sydney for the Royal Easter Show. Then I know the people of New South Wales. Before then I was lost, I don't know what to do, lost in my father's memory, I was remembering. When he went to hospital, Darwin hospital, I was there and then he said to me,
    "The time is come, son,
    take my heart, take my word,
    take my courage.
    I am handing over to you because I am no longer with you,"
and then he passed away.
    "I am just telling you very strongly,
    take my heart,
    take my word, take my memory with you.
    No matter whoever they hate you, don't take notice,
    help them, tell them the story.
    One day the Balanda going to come and destroy the land."

That was true. He didn't know, but he ***know*** what would happen in Yirrkala. The big meeting come – all the Parliament from Canberra tried to tell us, what to say, how to build the road, how to dig the mine, how to protect one area but if not it would get worse and worse. Then someone was coming from Melbourne, Frank Purcell and John Little and K.C. Woodward. They came down to Yirrkala and try to help us get the land back 'cause my own Methodist missionary head office is in Sydney and they sell the land: we didn't know.

As I was telling you all the big bosses from Canberra, the Parliament, visit us at Yirrkala and they tell us and talk to us, making agreement. They saying this word, "Well, old people" (they all gone now, my old people, only few left, old man). Anyhow they was talking to us, "OK, leaders of the different clans, we like to build a little township."

We thought, just a little one is it,
but they are tricking us.
We thought, just a little one is it,
but they are tricking us.
We thought just a little township like we have now in
      different part of Arnhem Land on homeland centre,
but they start bring bulldozer, factory, machine to clearing
      road, to clearing area for bauxite,
and the township was growing bigger and bigger and bigger,
and we were very surprised and we start opening our eyes
      and ears
because no one ever been able to tell us what going
      to happening.
Even my own missionary, not tell to the Yolŋu, no one.

Then we had a big meeting because they knock a special
      tree at Wallaby Beach, a big banyan.
They knock one special tree, the Wuyal's tree.
Everybody was unhappy, because that's the tree, most
      important one.

*The second bark petition sent to the
Australian Parliament in 1968.*

*Bark painting by Jackie Dundiwuy
Wanambi of Wuyal, the ancestral man
who created many sacred sites in the
Nhulunbuy area. Wuyal is carrying his
stone axe and wears a madayin object
around his neck. His shovel nose spear
and woomerah are beside him.*

Then I made up my mind, I tell all the people, what the old people taught us, my father Galarrwuy's father, and Gawerin's father, old man which is my grandfather, my father's mother's brother. I was talking to some others too, Gumatj, Djapu, Madarrpa, Maŋgalili and Djambarrpuyŋu tried to talk to them. "What shall we do" and we trying hard, we push ourselves very strongly to Land Rights case in Darwin in 1971.

We make up our mind ourself to go through and do to get the land right back and that why I meet Jenny Isaacs because she is the Land Rights secretary with Dr Coombs. He went there to Yirrkala with Jenny and with Jean Battersby, because they work together in one office, and they help us.

Then, in 1972 I had a letter from Melbourne from lawyer. I tried to find somebody to help us, and I did, I found it – the lawyers Frank Purcell and John Little was flown over to Yirrkala especially to visit me to talk to me how I feel about this land.

Frank Purcell and John Little and K.C. Woodward came to Yirrkala tried to help Yolŋu to get the land back.

      That what he, Frank Purcell, was asking. He said to me,
      "How you feel about this mine all over your land?
      Are we going to make a court case to try to get your land
            back, or what do you think?"

Sacred mawalan decorated with ḻindirritj feathers, sent to Canberra during the historic Rirratjiṅu Land Rights struggle.

And I was very surprised.
"OK", I said, "we'll try to get our land back."
Yirrkala is the first, we push ourselves very strongly,
try to get our land back, and we push ourselves into Land
    Right case in Darwin, that is the first land right case.
But we already have a problem because they destroy one
    special tree,
and also at Mt Saunders, Nhulunbuy they destroy the hill,
the spirit home of Wuyal, sugarbag man,
to make the water tank for the township.

Then I said,
"OK, I need help. I just been talk to all on behalf of my
    people to get the land back."
OK and we have a big discussion and make everything ready,
the sacred object,
the sacred dilly bag,
We are against Commonwealth Law,
take all our sacred object, decoration for the land
and show them, especially Djaŋkawu object,
Djaŋkawu maḏayin.
The land is most important to us,
and I am the man who made the sacred object,
but they have been make big mistake in name,
but doesn't matter, no matter, whatever.

I am me, I am Wandjuk, but it must be my name on the
    Land Right case,
because I was the man to organise the sacred things,
the sacred object,
and make the sacred object or mawalan
the names, Mawalan names
and Wawilak names
and Djaŋkawu names.
And then in 1972 he made a date.
In 1972 I get all the people, old people and we went to
    Darwin for the Land Rights case.

That was my first step to see the Balanda's world, to talk the Balanda language against the Balanda Commonwealth law, on the Land Rights case. That my first step, to see, to talk a different tongue. I can talk from my own heart and my own mind. Nobody told me how to talk, what word put into mind or to my tongue, to talk to Balanda. That was in 1972. I take the sacred object to that Land Right case and I bring all the big bosses, like the Barrister, K.C. Woodward, Judge Blackburn and some other Queen's solicitors and the old people, my own people. We were there in that courtroom, and we show them that these things very important, and we explain to them.

Above: *Wandjuk Marika travelled to Perth to attend the opening of the Berndt Museum of Anthropology at the University of Western Australia.*

Right: *Wandjuk Marika at a formal occasion in Yirrkala.*

Far right: *Wandjuk Marika, OBE.*

I say to them,
"Hey, you can see these special feathers and special
    sacred object.
This is for the land – decoration.
The land is full of this,
land is not empty, land is not empty.
These, the land decoration, we show you,
and we proving you because you think we have nothing.
The song, the ceremony, is come from this one, the sacred."
I was saying that in the courtyard, inside the court room.

I was a man who pushed myself very hard against government law to make the Balanda understanding what the culture and what the land, how we love the land, because our land is most important and special because our land is from the Creation, because our land is the mother. The land have many things, power, experience and knowledge. That's what I explain to the government – to show them the land decorations, so they can understand.

I found many letter or picture the Balanda thought which has crept in from Asian country, the Pacific to the land here. They thought we just made a story. The Balanda thought we just made up story. How could we know?
    We know the trees, the land and the dancing is came from
        the land,
    song and ceremony is came from the land.
    I was talking and explaining this to them.

    And then we miss everything.
    We miss, lost the Land Rights case.

Then later I push myself, bring all things from Yalaŋbara to the Land Right case, belong to Yalaŋbara. Yalaŋbara is mine – leader or head of the ceremony, and also Yalaŋbara is a winner. First we miss, second we miss, but third, we got it.

We get the Land Right back 1977, when I was been Chairman for Aboriginal Arts Board of Australia Council. Otherwise it would have been nothing. Now, we lucky, everybody going out to establish their own tribal land, what we call homeland. Used to be outstation, but it is not outstation, outstation is for cattle station, now we call ours homelands. We working by ourselves now – no boss about it. Aboriginal to Aboriginal so we can understand each other, our own language instead of just Balanda come and told what to do, where to go, what to find.

Chairman, Aboriginal Arts Board of the Australia Council.

Before that I been travelling around the world with World Council of
Churches, and then I got more ideas about how to help, how to stand
for the land or talk for the land to explain to them about many
things what Yolŋu know.

Now we lucky we got it,
thanks for these things that have been done, work,
    hard work.
I was been working for the land right declaration,
and when I was in Canberra with the children I saw that
    walking stick is there in Parliament House, Canberra,
which is the one I take up into the land right court case.
When I saw that walking stick, name after my father
I was crying,
remind me way back,
remind me the beginning.
And that is the history, I have, in Canberra.

When I saw that I was crying,
not only me, but my children was crying,
my children was with me, remind me that I have been strug-
    gling for the land with *that* decoration,
made by my father,
he made it – string, special feathers,
and also the walking stick.
And now I am free and happy to move back to the place
    to Yalaŋbara,
which is the Yalaŋbara, which is top,
and winner for the Land Right.

This is my story and my life story, which is happen.
First of all I was learn of the land from my father.
Sometime I used to go to the bush,
away from Mum and Dad for 12 months.
They used to worry about me in the bush, sometimes frighten.
I go by myself with some friends
and learn about the natural things, nature, the life we share
    with my own people,
the life that we began,
that Balanda don't know.
Yes, it's land, it's land, but what's *in* it,
Balanda doesn't know what's in it, how to go about.
Even Balanda might go bush for two or three days, he'll
    be finished.
I can go 26 days without food, without water,
but I know, I know.
I fight very strongly to get the land back and get money.

PAINTING

NOTES

Wandjuk composed this chapter in 1984 at a time when he was feeling disillusioned, having put so much effort into working with the Balanda community. In the early 1980s the Aboriginal Arts Board moved towards increasing representation and funding for urban Aboriginal artists. The emphasis had shifted away from negotiating and working with traditional people. When he visited the Arts Board office he noticed no one from the north to whom he could relate well.

In the intervening ten years this changed. Wandjuk's sister, Banduk Mamburra Marika chaired the Aboriginal Visual Arts Committee of the Australia Council for a time. Mamburra makes linocut prints, many of which reinterpret the traditional Djaŋkawu and Wawilak stories.

Paintings are not simply works of art. They may be compared to sacred scripts – documents which detail the spiritual origins of mankind, the creatures of the earth and the physical form of nature. Mawalan handed onto Wandjuk the full repertoire of Rirratjiŋu design custodianship, and taught him the skills to execute the paintings. In turn, Wandjuk trained his eldest son, Mawalan II.

Painting is very important.
It's the design or symbol, power of the land.
First I learned to paint when I was a young man
from my father, Mawalan,
when he take me though the bush, teaching me
where to go, where to find, what to hunt
and the special places.
Then I learnt Yolŋu writing, my own designs,
drawing on the rock or on the sand
and then putting in the hatching.
I start on the bark maybe when I was about 15 years of age.
But my father was still holding my hand.
I used to shake my hand, but he was holding it.
And he always said to me, "Hold your brush straight,
paint away from your body. Use your wrist with the brush.
Just put the line there. Most important is the line.
Most important is the animal you draw," he said to me.

He still talks to me today,
how to record
and put the line straight and true.

After two months he let me go by myself,
he was still watching.
I sit with bark on my lap, or on the ground,
and then he's holding my hand, helping me with the brush,
rest a bit so the cross-hatching can dry.

I see the designs on my body
paint on for a circumcision first, to make me young man,
but, before that, I saw some other people who painted them
on other bodies when they first come to Yirrkala for
    special ceremonies,
like Djaŋkawu ceremony,

110

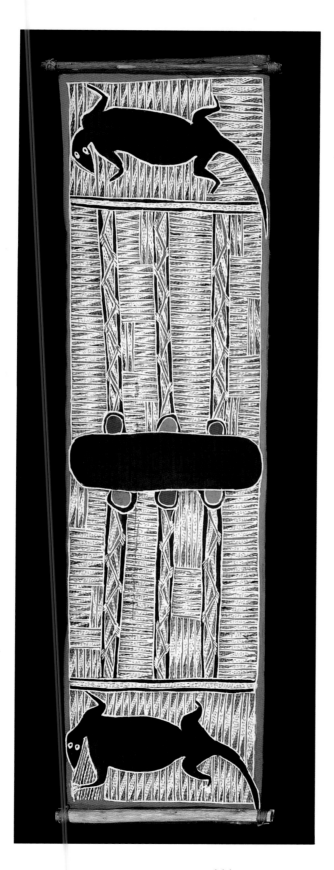

Bark painting by Wandjuk Marika, 1982.

The Dwelling Place of the Goannas.

"The black mark in the middle of this painting, that's the rock, which you can still see today. See these six holes, you can see the track going into the hole where the goanna rested in the night, then next morning on the other side they were going up. When the evening comes, the goanna again comes down and goes into the hole again. Next morning they do the same thing, and you can see all the scratching marks of the goanna – the sand falling down as they are playing around."
– Wandjuk Marika, 1984.

Top: *Visit of art collector Dr Scougall
(left), Margaret and Tony Tuckson from
the Art Gallery of NSW and Dorothy
Bennett (right) to Yirrkala, 1959.
The artists gathered are from left:
Gunyalawuy, Mataman, Mungurrawuy,
Muditpuy, Wandjuk and his father
Mawalan.*

Above: *Wandjuk (rear) and
Mungurrawuy (left) explain the meaning
of a painting to Tony Tuckson from the
Art Gallery of NSW, 1959.*

or for special burial,
and on special objects.
For my circumcision that's when I began to learn stories,
men came from many areas.
They sang manikay (songs) and made dances.
I was not allowed to talk to mother,
only allowed to talk to father, cousin or brother,
or the grandmother or grandfather,
but not to the mother, mother's brother or my
    sister's husband
not allowed to talk to them while I'm learning.
I used to go to these ceremonies until I became
    more knowing
about the song and painting.
Then my father said, "You can talk now, OK,
you are handling the ceremony now you can talk to mother,
    mother's brother and sister's husband."
Now after that, that's why I know more detail
    about painting,
not only Djaŋkawu painting, also Wawilak,
and sacred story belong to Yirrkala, Seagull.

In my first start, I do paintings with my father,
learning paintings, work together.
Like we have a big bark there and he was teaching me
and we work together.
He was painting the line first and then he let me,
to see how I might handle the brush, if I was shaking, or if
    I was steady.
He was watching me at the same time.
He do it
and then he watching my line
and I watching his.
Some of those paintings are together in Brisbane,
    Melbourne and Sydney Art Galleries.

While I was a teacher's assistant in school,
maybe 15 or 16 years of age,
then this strange new idea was coming into mind.
Then I mix, use four colour, red, black, yellow and **green**.
Where did I get the green?
I mix the black and yellow!
My father was very cross at me. And then he said
"Where did you get this mulmu (green grass) colour?"
I said, "From my own mind",
and he said, "Forget it."
So I did,
but then I see, I'm laughing now,

112

those mulmu paintings are in the Art Gallery of New
South Wales!
I didn't see them for 20 years.

Also, at the same time,
I drew on the paper to make a modern water colour,
that was in the school, and for Professor Berndt.
My father saw that and said "Yaka! (No!)
Do our way. Just copy, there and there, and there,
you going to be a good artist."

My father taught me many things.
The Djaŋkawu are the Creation ancestors. They travelled,
making waterholes, creating all the tribes,
    children, languages.
I am the man,
descended from the Djaŋkawu, the man himself,
seven, eight thousand generations ago.

I was painting with my father at Yirrkala until about 1963 or 64. Mr
and Mrs Tony Tuckson and Dr Scougall and Dorothy Bennett – we
made an exhibition to be opened up by my father.

He travelled to Sydney wearing special clothes.[15]
I was making very special arm bands for him
to show the world the culture and law of our people.

Yes, Tony Tuckson got those paintings and before that another lot
came and they also made a movie, about fishing and drawing in the
sand. I don't remember who that was, I think the Institute,
Australian Aboriginal Institute.[16] The Balanda and missionaries was
collecting all the bark and I work on stories. Then they said to me,
"OK, Wandjuk, your time has come. You're going to travel to different part of world, because you are very important and have had more
experience, have more knowledge, can understand your culture and
our culture very clearly, and we want you to be travelling." I wouldn't
believe what they were telling me. Were they pulling my leg or was it
just a story? I thought they just making fun of me, that what I was
thinking first place. Then I tell myself the Balanda world is a strange
world, but, anyhow, I will have to try hard. So I'm working and working all night, painting everything. I'm lucky to have the experience. I
have the knowledge to talk, the power to talk.

*Wandjuk and his father Mawalan
stripping bark from eucalyptus trees
(Eucalyptus tetradonta). Very large
pieces were collected to make paintings
for the Art Gallery of New South
Wales, 1959.*

---

15 He was naked, wearing no shirt, only a naga (loin cloth), ceremonial armband, beard
    feathers and a feather belt.
16 Australian Institute of Aboriginal and Torres Strait Islander Studies.

My first trip was down to Sydney. There was the Royal Easter Show. That was my first visit to the city, because I'm an artist, and I found the famous son, famous artist's son, Albert Namatjira's son, Keith Namatjira. Albert Namatjira and my father, Mawalan, are the most famous artists of all. Albert Namatjira is a famous artist for modern paint, water colour, and my father, Mawalan, is a famous artist on traditional art, and we, their sons, meet each other in Sydney. We work together for two weeks, yes, I think two weeks in Sydney, at the Showground, where we did the painting at the same time the Royal Easter Show.

When the stringybark is removed it curls back to the shape of the tree and must be thinned, flattened and seasoned, 1959.

My father passed away in 1967 in Darwin Hospital.
He was very sick and the doctor said to me,
"OK, your father is not going to get better",
but he [the doctor] is trying hard.
"He's half and half" he said, the doctor said to me.
"He's half and half,
I don't know whether he going to get better or whether he
    going to be gone."
It is true. The doctor was very good to my father.
The doctor said to me, "Don't worry we will do our very best
    to make your father better."

And then my father said to me,
"Look, Wandjuk, my son, I'm no longer with you.
I have passed it all on to you.
You have to think hard
and learn about many ways.
Take my stick [djuta],
take my word,
take my energy,
take my courage.
One day the Balanda, they will come and destroy our land,
but I'm not going to see what is going to happen,
so you have to stand tall to talk for our land,
for your children,
for your children's children.
Doesn't matter whatever, whether black or white,
if they're going to hate you, don't take notice of
    them seriously,
just talk kindly and sensibly."
Then he passed away the same night, and I was sad for
    two years.

Then in 1969
I started the ceremony to make myself free,
ready for the big battle.
Not battle with the spear, but battle for the land.

114

*Bark painting by Wandjuk Marika, 1982.
Mururruma.*

*Mururruma is one of the great songmaker
ancestors of the Rirratjiŋu. After his violent
death he became a huge rock which stands
in the sea near Yirrkala (the black shape is
the submerged part of the rock, the white
is above the sea). Mururruma's spirit is
standing on that rock. A storm rages
around him. The vertical yellow lines are
the lightning, the vertical hatchings the
thunder, the horizontal hatchings the rain
clouds and the diagonals surrounding the
figure are the rain. On either side of the
vertical yellow lines is a rough sea.*

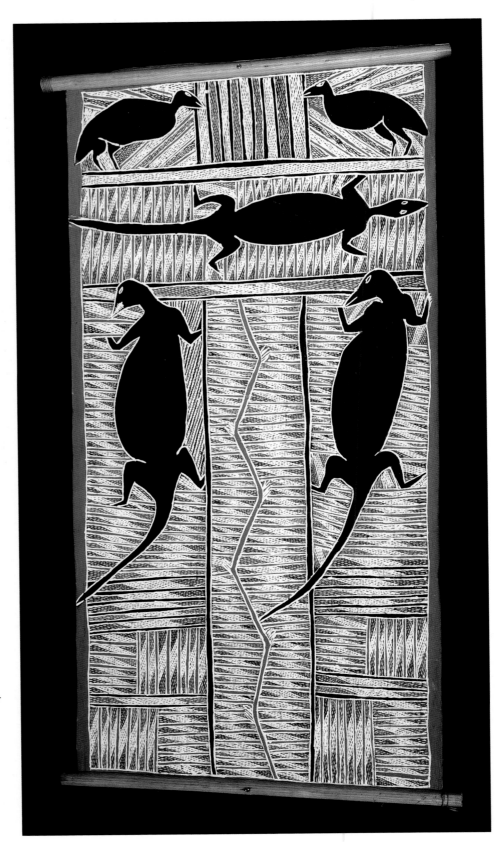

Bark painting by Wandjuk Marika,
1982.
Goannas and Bustards.

*The centre panel of this picture is the
tracks of djanda, the goanna. On either
side a goanna looks towards the sea.
The patterns below the tails represent
the sand falling down the dunes as they
climb. Another goanna (top centre) is
lying across the rock which is their
home. The two bush turkeys, buwaṯa,
are moving through the scrub to the
succulent brown berries, a favourite
food depicted as the vertical hatchings.*

Not a big battle with gun or the spear,
but I make myself dhuŋ (to stand up for my rights),
sharp as a knife or spear or gun,
get ready, make myself strong.
Otherwise I would have ended as a slave and unworthy.

In 1970 I was appointed member of Australian Council for the Arts, and then I became Chairman, after Dick Roughsey, of Aboriginal Arts Board.

So there was a big election in 1973, Yolŋu from different part of Australia. They had a big seminar in Canberra, in 1973. All the tribal and urban Aboriginals come together to Canberra for big ceremony for same, and then we created Aboriginal Arts Board of the Australia Council. Used to be Australian Council for the Arts, that's where Jennifer Isaacs was working as a Secretary for land and for very own land rights, Australian Council for the Arts. From there in 1973, we come together and create the new name that we have today – Aboriginal Arts Board of the Australia Council. I was the first member of that for three years – 1973, 74 and 75.

In 1973 I become a member of Aboriginal Arts Board of Australia Council and all Yolŋu from the different Pacific islands and from Australia and Mornington Island came to Opera House opening and we sitting VIP seat and I was nervous. I was sitting in a very important seat. We saw the Queen. I saw the Queen, 1973, also 1981. Other Yolŋu working at Aboriginal Arts Board – there was Albert Barunga, David Mowaljarlai, Larry Lanley and Bobby Barjarai, somebody from Oenpelli or Maningrida, and many more, I forget about the names. Also there was the Aboriginal singer, Harold Blair, Chikka Dixon, the southern Aboriginal. I'll try to remember the others. Only those people I remember.

When I was a member Dick Roughsey was Chairman of the Aboriginal Arts Board, and then we working, start to travel. In the same year, 1973, I fly over to Moscow, or Russia, that was my first **out** from Australia. I see the different country and mix with the white society, I was in Russia for three weeks, then I flew back home to Australia, and I start working.

That was my time to see,
to work for the Aboriginal people in the white society.
I understand about the two ways.
I was trying help the people setting up their
    own organisations,
like Aboriginal hostels, Aboriginal schools and
    Aboriginal hospitals.

Top: *Wandjuk's father Mawalan Marika painting in 1959.*

Above: *Completing a major painting for the Art Gallery of NSW. Wandjuk Marika (left) works with his father and others, 1959.*

And then it was not long and they have one,
they have many things.
Working themselves,
because I been encouraging them,
give them understanding.
I told them because they have been lost in the first place,
we are lucky now.
But still they do not say "Thanks" or send me letter.

Also I've been setting up Aboriginal Arts and Crafts, that used to be.
It's changed now. Then I was travelling in New Guinea, it was about
1974, and help the people there, for the cultural exchange. I take the
group of people, the dances there, and we meet each other as black to
black, brothers and sisters. We were there for maybe a week, then we
fly back home. We landed in Cairns.

That was 1974.

Then I walked into one of the shops and I found the
    tea towel,
published in Holland,
which had my own sacred design on this tea towel,
    table cloth.
When I walk into that shop, and when I saw it
I was shocked and break my heart.

I bought it, cost me maybe $10
and then I said to the shopkeeper,
"Look you don't charge me that much.
This is my own design, you have no right to sell it.
This is bad. This is my own design, my sacred design.
I will only buy that for $2, just for the cloth,
because it's my own copyright design."

Then I was thinking very hard.
What shall I do, where shall I get the help,
who's going to help to stop this copyright stealing?
Instead of painting their own painting, they always
    copy designs
from the traditional areas.

They don't know what the painting is.
They thought they are just pleasure paintings
but it's the symbol, the power, experience and knowledge.
After I found my own design on the tea towels I was shocked
and I lose my power to paint,
lose my power for a number of years.

*Wandjuk's father Mawalan Marika pauses
while painting at Raŋi, 1959.*

Yes, I was thinking and thinking;
I try and try and at last something was coming into
    my mind.
Ah, I said, I have to send this to the Prime Minister,
the former Prime Minister, which is Gough Whitlam.
Gough was Labor Prime Minister,
and I sent the two towels to Canberra to Prime Minister
and I say, "OK, I need help to setting up something to
    protect the copyright.
I need the lawyer or someone",
and they say to me "OK. Don't worry Wandjuk, we'll
    help you."
And now I've got it.
Aboriginal Artists Agency Copyright Council.
And there's another thing too about the Arts and Crafts.
I was talking to the missionaries to get building
so we can work as Aboriginal Arts and Crafts shop,
in our own lands,
on our home.
I did. I got it.
Aboriginal Arts and Crafts in Yirrkala.

Not only that,
but I have been trying to help the different arts
in all parts of Australia –
all parts of Australia – even the south
because I'm artist.
I'm travelling right round Australia
to see and to help.

It was been very hard for me and very difficult,
but I help through working and setting up
no matter whoever they are.
Then I become a retired Board member,
and today, now it is changed.
Many things have changed,
because in the Aboriginal Arts Board Australia Council
no tribal Aboriginals working there now,
only southern people.

*Mawalan holds a major descriptive painting
of the actions of the Creation Ancestors of
the Rirratjiŋu, including the Djaŋkawu's
journey in the canoe from Burralku and the
appearance of the Thunderman,
Djambuwal, 1959.*

At the same time, we start making road to Port Bradshaw, Yalaŋbara, and then I fly back to the meeting again, and I was been working, helping to discuss many things. Then in 1975 I become Chairman of Aboriginal Arts Board of Australia Council. When I was become Chairman, then the government recognise me, they gave me reward, then I received an award, an OBE, because I'm artist, because I do many things in Balanda world. I was been Chairman, 75, 76, 77, 78, 79 – five years. 73, 74, 75 I was a member, and then middle, round

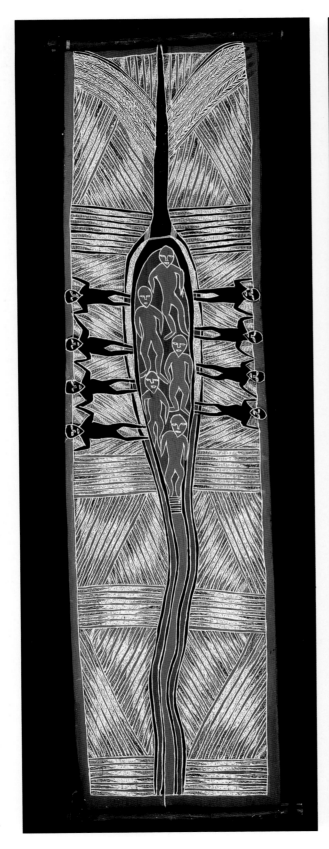

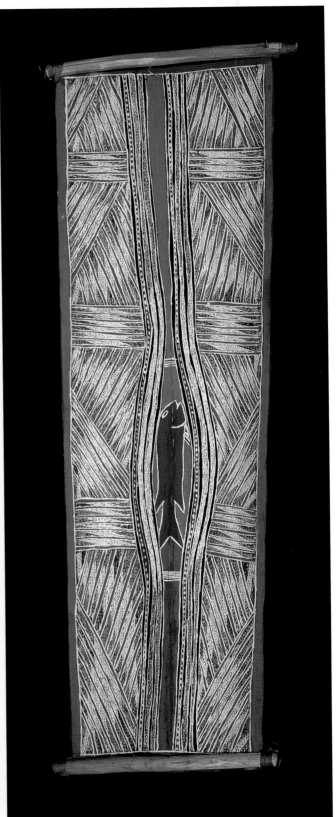

about October, I became Chairman. Not only that, when I was been Chairman, I been travelling different part of world, Balanda world – United States. I flew over to New Mexico, Albuquerque, we take exhibition to people there. Before that I fly over to Nigeria, Africa, we setting up the cultural exchange arts world, Festac, Festival of Arts for all the black countries of the world. I setting it up and then I fly back home to Australia. 1976 I was fly over to another Pacific Festival in New Zealand or cultural exchange or whatever name is. All the tribal Aboriginal people, from different part of north Australia, not south end, but from top end, like Maningrida, Bamyili and Tiwi and Yirrkala. We have a big festival there from different parts of world – the South Pacific Festival.

> When I meet an Aboriginal or southern Aboriginal, they
>   always crying
> and they will turn to me and say to me, "Please,
>   tribal brother,
> we have been lost.
> Could you help us?
> Give us more understanding about our culture.
> Give us more knowledge to call ourselves Aboriginal."
> And then I said to them,
> "Don't worry, you're not a southern Aboriginal,
> you're not a half caste, quarter caste.
> You live in cold country – that's why your skin is brown.
> I am a full blood because I am from tribal area and
>   hot country
> from the top of Australia.
> Don't worry, I will help you, time is come.
> This is my time to see, to work for the Aboriginal in
>   the white society."

I been understanding about the two ways. I been trying help the people to setting up their own organisations, like Aboriginal hostels, Aboriginal schools and Aboriginal hospitals. And then, it was not long and they have one, they have many things. Working themselves, because I been encourage them. Give them understanding.

> I told them because they have been lost in the first place.
> We are lucky, now, but still they don't say me "thanks" or
>   send me letter.

Then I had my exhibition in 1982, I decide to raise money, get the rupiah for Yalaŋbara. In Melbourne I paint all the story, Djaŋkawu, Wawilak, Mururruma. Took me six months, very hard work.

> But I get the power back.
> It is very peaceful there with my little girl and Jenny Home.

Wandjuk with Jenny Home and their daughter Mayaṯili at Wandjuk's solo exhibition, Hogarth Galleries, Sydney 1982.

"That exhibition made me feel strong, happy." – Wandjuk Marika.

Opposite: *Bark paintings by Wandjuk Marika, 1982.*

The Wawilak Sisters.

Two Wawilak sisters travelled from Trial Bay across to the Arafura Sea. The younger sister was pregnant when they reached the Mirramina waterhole where the Rainbow Snake lived. The Snake reared out of the water and swallowed the younger sister and her unborn child. Other great snakes came to ask the cause of the commotion and when he confessed to his action the monsoon began to rage. He fell to earth with such force that the ground split making a river. After this he regurgitated the younger sister and her baby.

The painting on the left depicts part of the Wawilak ceremony performed today

In the painting on the right the monsoonal rain created by the Rainbow Snake is represented by the hatching. A rifle fish swims in the raging river.

Wandjuk at his solo exhibiton, Sydney, 1982. Many of the paintings which were exhibited, and which appear in this book, were purchased by the National Gallery of Australia, Canberra.

She always come to me and watch me.
One painting take may be a week or two,
very fine line,
very fine and straight, not shaking.
These are most important design,
symbol for the land and I decide to have the exhibition for
        selling paintings to get the rupiah.
But not for Balanda to buy them, put on their wall or
        whatever –
it's for all the people, so they can **learn**,
black and white together.
I wanted an Art Gallery to buy them, and they did,
Australian National Gallery, Canberra.

Yes, but there is the money problem. Nobody ever share sunset to sun-rise together, we work together all right but no money sharing. Now I start to thinking what shall I do. Now I am working by myself, with my own eye, with my own hand. I have the successful exhibition. Then I get the money – all the painting different. Before that my paintings were sent but I never got royalties, no way in the world, nobody ever really recognise me for my special painting. If you want to go there you can see in New South Wales State Art Gallery, there is a hundred of my paintings. I never get the royalty or recognition for that. I try to get the help, but nothing. Now I am looking after my family. Even the royalty I did not get for Yalaŋbara, for Yalaŋbara names. Now I'm moving out because I got the money from exhibition.

I'm moving back to my land to work, to settle down,
    to raise money.
I'm the freedom man.
Nobody going to tell me what to do, where to go, how
    to work,
but I'm going to do what I want to do.
This is the book I'm written, my life story.

Many years I have not been able to do any painting, but now this is my time, and now I have had an exhibition in 1982, and all the painting going into my book. We put the exhibition in Hogarth Gallery, Sydney – my own exhibition – filled it up with the paintings. We took over that gallery, paid the rent, so I could make more rupiah – not give the commission or I might lose more.

That exhibition made me feel strong, happy. The family came from home to see those stories and learn. Wukaka I and some others. Then I got it, may be $15,000, and we bought the Toyota to go to Yalaŋbara move the family there from Yirrkala, away from the drinking.

The paintings are very special and very important.

Balanda and southern Aboriginals can learn now
and see
because this is the very special and very
    important knowledge
that nobody ever knew as I did.
The anthropologists can't do this way.
They can write the book,
but not from their mind.
They have been seeing the people for two or three weeks
and then they go home, go back to their office
and they work and write from the Balanda history,
not from the Yolŋu history.
This is **my** own history,
the Yolŋu history,
especially from north-eastern Arnhem Land.
There is many more written,
but this is the translation of these paintings.
So, painting have meaning;
painting have a story;
not just painting, ordinary painting.

I'm doing my book for my children,
not only for my children but for different part of the world;
different part of Australia;
not only for the tribal area but also for the southern area,
because I know how much I have learnt –
the painting, the meaning.
I am not painting just for my pleasure,
there is the meaning, knowledge and power.
This is the earthly painting for the Creation
and for the land story.
The land is not empty,
the land is full of knowledge,
full of story,
full of goodness,
full of energy,
full of power.
Earth is our mother,
the land is not empty –
there is the story I am telling you –
special, sacred, important.

*"Painting is very important, it's the symbol,
the power, experience, knowledge."*
– Wandjuk Marika

NOTES

There are various techniques of care for the body and spirit available in Yolŋu culture. Wandjuk was always interested in aspects of Balanda medicine that approximated his own. Most Yolŋu responded early to the effectiveness of simple remedies such as aspirin and acknowledged the effect of antibiotics. Direct physical intervention in health, for example through injections, correlates with important aspects of Yolŋu healing, such as massage which Wandjuk calls "rubbing", and the application of herbal compresses. Numerous plants are also used to make infusions which may be inhaled or sipped.

The various specialties of Yolŋu healing fall to different skilled people; some are herbalists while others practise what Wandjuk calls "mind medicine". Mind medicine can involve using objects such as the "magic" stones from sacred sites of ancestors that are imbued with certain power, but it also involves skilled practice and processes not recounted here. A great deal of Wandjuk's influence among Yolŋu stemmed from his knowledge of these practices as an adjunct to his ceremonial and ancestral leadership.

Wandjuk attributed our long and close friendship to his early use of this mind medicine. In the early months of our association and as part of my adoption as a Warramiri (octopus woman), sister of his wives, Gotjiriŋu and Dhuwandjika, he presented me with beautiful and mysterious malarrami pebbles. We had not mentioned them for many years but when we reached this section of the book I found them once again. He was not surprised to see them in my possession 15 years later and he said "Yes, Galay, of course, you are still here and I am still here. They are strong."

BALANDA AND YOLŊU MEDICINE

There are two ways, Balanda medicine and Yolŋu, Balanda medicine is sometimes getting manymak (good) for your body, and also for your feeling, or even injection and some kind of disprins or cough mixture, sometime getting manymak, sometime getting worse. Because the Yolŋu drink, drinking and drinking, drinking – more, what you call blood pressure – because the Yolŋu yaka (don't) care for themselves, or care their body, and their body get worse There's the other thing too – operation. Balanda can changing their natural body, the body of Yolŋu, use the heart from any animals or get the other blood from the other person who have nothing blood. So that you can live a bit longer.

Then, the second way is Yolŋu,
Yolŋu medicine, Yolŋu way is for when **I** get sick
and you have to get some special bush medicine for
    your headache
or for your toothache.
When you have a bad feeling or your back aching a lot
and then Yolŋu have to make a fire, a hot fire
and get the pandanus nut, also the lily and räkay grass,
pick 'em up from the swamp and mix with the mud,
then we make it hot, not a really hot, but warm,
and cover with that räkay's leaves
make warm and cover with paperbark,
across your back, rubbing your back maybe for one and a
    half hours.
You're lying there until you're getting very sweaty all round
    your face
and then you take the paperbark off your body
and then after that it will be rubbing you with warm sand,
    not hot,
or you might get burnt, get blister everywhere on your body,
and then rubbing you –
then you just get well and fit again.

Top: *Yolŋu medicinal plants: pandanus fruit, and* (above) *swamp lily tubers are mashed and used to make a strong antiseptic and healing liquid.*

Opposite: *Wandjuk Marika sitting outside the house at Raŋi, 1972.*

127

Wandjuk's granddaughter Maxine with his sister Banduk, among the Räkay grass near Yirrkala. The stems are used for "steaming" medicine and the corms are edible.

I have the same thing done to me
I was fall down from tree and hurt my back,
or maybe my bone is crack or slip
and then my mother is make the fire to covering me
    with the warm sand
and mat and that räkay grasses, warm grass.
Then I not been able to be sick.

Once I was **sick**.
I just lay down on the hot sun to make myself warm again
or make myself feel better,
or sometime I drink salt water,
instead of cough mixture or whatever the
    Balanda medicine,
or rubbing.
We have to get a special, what you call it, squid's back.
We call that galpawiri, rubbing it on your back and you get
    manymak.
Yes, you use that galpawiri for any kind of pain
and also I have a special kind of Warramiri things,
    malarrami – *eyes of the octopus* –
and that's why I'm always well and strong.

I used to be sick every day or even out driving.
I was always getting ache in my back and my shoulder
and I always get that eyes of octopus from Wessel Islands.
It's a rock, a special area which is my mother's totem to care
    for me, look after me
and if I put that thing around my body or organ, make
    me strong.
If I feel like I'm going to have a drink, cup of tea, for make
    me strong.
I have to put that rock into the tea pot,
not the tea pot but the cup,
put it there for about ten minute, take it off and drinking it.
When you drink that tea after you take it off the rock
    tastes salt
instead of just tea tastes salt because octopus is a salt,
good and very dangerous.
Yes the stones is Creation.

Märrma (two) way – octopus and also that rock malarrami
    or Bandaŋuwami, is a sacred site of octopus, mända
and we still have that there,
and also there is a special jungle, and octopus live right in
    the hollow log.
When you go and knock the hollow, this octopus change
    into flying fox,

in Gurrarama, in Wessel Islands, my mother's country
which is very strong Warramiri totem and symbol.

Some of the young people living there.
The father was there, probably you know him or heard
    about him.
He is there.
Yes, that's the one now, name is Djiŋulul No. 1.
Like you have manikay (song) for Christmas – Jingle Bell,
    Jingle Bell.
That his name, Djiŋulul,
and also his son is there now and his wife and mother of
    that old man.

Then there is the stone, milirrk,
that's not the medicine, but the magic,
what I've been know since about 19 years of age,
and then my mind was working,
sometime I used to in a dream (not really in a dream but in
    the night)
I have been fly away just like a superman.
I used to fly different part of world.
I used to fly in the night
and see back home with that one,
milirrk,
see what going on, what happening there,
and I still do the same thing,
but this time my mind is going back to home and I know
    whoever the person passed away,
and every time I ring back home, and ask them what going
    on what happening,
nobody ever told me but I always ask them what going
    on there,
who passed away.
Sometime I used to ask, "Is it so and so, is passed away?"
I mention name and they always answer "Yes."
"You know why," I always say.
But still I can see what going on there.
Before I was been mixed up, miyalk (woman) and
    ŋänitji (drink),
but this time I am clear myself, so I can see clearly,
instead of being mixed.

Well, the milirrk that's my symbol and that's my magic
but only the individual person who is the owner of that land
    is allowed to pick up.
Before you pick it up you have to talk and put the sweat.
Yes, it is danger, and it's OK,

you put sweat around and talk to it now and say this words
    to all that painting there, the lines there,
"It's OK, I'm going to take this one and protect myself from
    the danger",
and that's why all along I'm still alive.

Doesn't matter wherever I go, doesn't matter what I
    am doing,
that special magic is still in my body,
even someone is pointing to me a bone, a poison bone,
singing,
Maŋgi maŋgi is its name.
He just been nick me instead of going in,
or sometime he is going in to my body to touch the heart,
but that magic throw that away,
and sometime I tell them
"OK, somebody tricked me"
and I keep away from them
and I concentrate very hard to get my magic back,
and I did.
Three times or four times I been do it, when they try to
    destroy me.

Yes, the medicine.
The Yolŋu medicine and magic is stronger, but Balanda
    medicine is strong,
whether they make from tree or water or whatever, or
    mineral or whatever, turn into a medicine.

Balanda can make any medicine for a body.
For headache for anyone, Yolŋu or Balanda who have
    sickness on their heart aching or suffering from
    any illness.

But the Yolŋu can find some medicine from the bush and
    work on it.
Some Yolŋu have **mind** medicine,
and also there is the magic,
because the magic is come from the land,
not from tree or bush
(**they** have medicine not magic).

But the main one above all
is come from whoever created,[17] come from the special area,
special country to make better,
or make you see ways –
you can see what other people doing if they're travelling,

---

[17] Ancestors.

and how the other Yolŋu operating, keep
    themselves stronger.
Because we believe there is a medicine or a magic
and there is a power from the ***spiritual spirit.***

Some of the Yolŋu need magic get themselves stronger,
and when they have ***lost*** their magic they have to go to the
    Balanda doctor
to get the Balanda's medicine to help them to think clearly.
Sometime Balanda it work. And sometime it doesn't work:
that mean they have to go to the bush then
for three days by yourself,
sitting there and concentrate very hard,
[find] where's the power gone,
into that special area – talk to that area,
so the spirit of the earth, the feeling of the earth, it's come
    to you
and then you feel free, well and strong
and then you can hear the sound of that spirit,
not a bad spirit, but a good spirit.

The spirit belong to that land which is a most important
    creation,
like Yalaŋbara,
I have moved there,
I had so many struggling, so many bad habits,
then I move to live in my special area,
so I can get more power, more understanding,
have more feeling, kind and strongly and see the way
    very clearly,
because there is special feeling from the land.

BALANDA BRINGS BAD THING

NOTES

Wandjuk speaks briefly about things that affected Yolŋu deeply – racism, growing alcoholism in the community and the pervasive influence of Balanda culture, the way popular music and Christianity draw young people away from "Djaŋkawu manikay", the songs of Djaŋkawu.

Yes, there's a bad word Balanda say wherever he been go – "black" – that is the bad name or word say to Aboriginal. Yes, we are black, that is our natural colour. We born in black because we from top end, hot country.

From different part of Australia you can see brown skin yes, because they live on cold country or half and half, because they always married to Balanda. Those days that has been happening first settlers arrive in Australia and changing everything, married to the black.

Now it's the time, this time black man is married to a white woman, white man married to black girls, but still they called black. Black is like tar or the bitumen or any kind of paint, black paint, and that is the bad word and bad name to the Aboriginal people.
We are Aboriginal.
That is our own colour.
We didn't say to you, "White man" or "White chicken".

Long time ago when I start to look and see the Balanda.
At first I think – "What kind of monster,
wherever the eye or eyebrow, is it just a lump?
Doesn't look eye to eye – what wrong with them."
Then I get to know the Balanda well.

When I first go there in Darwin, the Yolŋu used to drink in the scrub, hiding themselves. Because Balanda doesn't want Yolŋu mob to be mix in the bar. I don't think that been happening now.

When the first mining company settled they built bar in Wallaby Beach, Melville Bay, or plant site. Yolŋu used to go and able to drink there, and Balanda used to say "Go away black bastard", which is yaka manymak, not so good word. Oh, many things like black, ignorant, stupid idiot, ignorant. Yes, dirty, filthy. That's the words they

used to say. Now, today, wherever I travel I did not hear any of that word as used to be. Why, even in Darwin they used to be hiding themselves in the scrub, sneaking, or maybe they used to give some money to Balanda, their friends, who used to go and get drink for them, then they drinking in the bush, but today nothing, we just drinking in the bar mixed with Balanda, and make ourselves friends.

We adopted Balanda to Yolŋu family, give them names, skinship and tribe, but before nothing have been happening like this, before. We are friendship, friends, and give the name or tribe or skinship. I think we doing very good now, not any bad feeling or hate each other, we come to be a friend – something is working for our children, now.

> The Balanda brought two thing.
> Good thing and bad thing.
> The bad thing they brought is drinking, alcoholic,
> and bring Yolŋu to Balanda way instead of Yolŋu way.
> The good thing, the good thing Balanda bring is Yolŋu
>   learn education,
> how to run their own affair or management,
> run by Yolŋu, like today.
> Everyone going out to their own tribal land to teach the
>   Yolŋu way,
> at the same time they learn more about the Christian way.
> We can't handling both Christian and traditional law.
> That is going to be very complicated for our children.

The teenage people they always play cassettes about the Elvis Presley. You can hear every night, every morning, wherever you can walk, hear the cassette or video or television. I don't know what his name – Presley – Elvis and some other cowboy song or disco song, or sometime they learning how to play the Balanda way, like guitars, all sorts of things – singing. But they learn more about the Balanda instead of our own way, and that's why I am writing this book, so they can able to see while they are young and learning all about their own culture and carry on for their children's children.

Maybe it's going to be happening very soon, but I do my best because young people have asked me to have a big ceremony, a special ceremony, to teach a different manikay, or different song, or different ceremony for individual tribe, because some of them eldest people are drinking gapu, ŋänitji (alcohol) but he's leader of the ceremony or the dancing or for the song. Yes, Balanda bring good thing and bad thing.

> I don't know, this my only time.
> I am thinking, and working

and I don't know what will be happening for the children
when they grow up to be a man and woman.

I have already been left somebody, someone,
some of the young boys
they always staying in Nhulunbuy for week and month
  and year,
they never come back,
they have a children,
they have a wife,
but they did not come back.

They always spending money on the liquor in Nhulunbuy, and they
come back and get more money from their wives, because they don't
know how to operating for work, what they going to do.

Some time girls, young girls, they always sleeping there, always staying in Nhulunbuy. There are even some, young boys and young
girls, in Darwin, but they don't know what they doing. They work
for the drink. They think drink give them more courage, more
knowledge, how to looking after themselves, but yaka – the drink
knocked them down.

Like I, myself, when I feel like I want a drink,
when I drink then I stop and think,
"What I'm doing, what will happening to me if I'm keep
  on drinking,
like the famous artist, Albert Namatjira, and all
  his children."
They are the famous artists, but they end up by drink,
end up by liquor, that's what I been thinking.

Sometime I'm going out, sometime I'm not feel
  like drinking.
I have to stop and think, to do, to work
and write the book for my children.

If I'm not going to do this thing, write the book as I am
  doing now,
what are my children going to learn?
Yes, because time is come, time is gone,
time is short and long.
Day go by and nothing more to stay a longer.

They don't know what they are doing. They thought that ŋänitji
drink is good but they don't know what is happening to them –
destroy their life. I think they all lose their mind, they got no way to

go, no way to operate. They always come back drunk, fighting with stick or knives or whatever, swearing, quarrelling. If they did not obey the Yolŋu law, we hand it over to the police, then they will give them warning so they won't be able to do more damage or fighting or whatever, because, as I said earlier, there's too much liquor, tape, cassette and video. Television, pushes their mind away from the Yolŋu.

> Sometime we can bring them back,
> to teach them more and talk to them.
> "Look," I always talk to them. "This is the law,
>   the foundation,
> you have to learn and stand on your feet.
> The Balanda come and go, they destroy your life."

> My little Mawalan used to be suffering,
> but good job he stop, and his brother.
> There's märrma (two) thing,
> TV and Christian – destroy.

Some of them, young people, become a pastor, a minister in the homeland, and there have been maybe about 220 people have been baptised. But own Christian law is Djaŋkawu manikay because it existed before the missionary arrive, used to be protecting us by the Djaŋkawu ceremony and Wawilak ceremony. Whenever they been committing adultery or murder or threatening or insulting to the other people, my father's father, my grandfather, used to make a ceremony about two Wawilak sisters to make them free and not make the trouble, to bring those murderers to be accepted as a family and now we got two ways now. Missionaries, they always say, "OK. This is your way and this is Christian way how about we can bring together – our two" but I don't know, they tried already, it will be very difficult for our young people to do the two ways. Not me. I'm still on old way of operating.

Yes, some of my family have become Christian, working on learning about the two ways. I think they going to be exactly the same as me. They can know two ways the Christian and our own law, but before that I only learn my own law, learn about our own culture *before* I got involved with the Balanda world and Balanda law.

> Some young people, my own race, Yolŋu
> they learn about Yolŋu culture and feeling just for a while.
> But then they go and have a drink,
> Balanda's poison.
> Kill the Yolŋu mind,
> kill the Yolŋu heart,
> kill the Yolŋu feeling.

Then they have lost their energy and their
    controlling themselves,
ŋänitji – they learn more about their Balanda way.
They thought ŋänitji [alcohol] is manymak
but it's part of a plant, like grapes
and then Balanda make it into a wine, or from all sorts
    of things
even from the cane, the sugar cane.
They drink but the Yolŋu don't know,
they thought it just make them happy and make them
    feel strong,
but it doesn't.
Some make themselves happy when they drink quietly,
like I used to drink, manymak gapu,
make you wise and you feel good.

Not long, I have a feeling when I been move up to country,
or to Melbourne, then I start drinking.
I have to do something to bring my feeling back,
because I been lost myself for eight years or ten years.
Do you know why I have been lost myself?
Because I found my tea towels which is published
and then I stopped painting for ten years.

Then I start to work on how I'm going to teach the young
    people, my children –
if I'm going to stay on same position of drinking,
go out, do what I want to do, make myself happy,
or make a pleasure for me some miyalk (woman) take me
    have a good time –
then I don't know anything.
Then I was stopped what I was doing.
I think, "I'll have to do something about my power before it
    too late."

My special boys, my boys bring me back,
they don't let me go into all these things,
but I need to go back and stay
and do what my parents, my spiritual peoples saying
not only my parents, but the magic and the spiritual spirit.

There are two spirits –
bad, puts you into the darkness,
tells you, "go about and make yourself happy",
but there is the other one, other spirit,
who can tell you, "come back, stay on one place and do
    something good –

And also I always feel angry and get wild because they
    always ask me
to say this and say that and do what I don't want to do,
and I said,
"Look, don't ever ask me to do that
look here, don't ever tell me,
I know how to speak the English, I know what to deal with,
I know how to mix
and Werner Herzog said, "Yes, I know but I'm from
    different country."
"What does it matter what different country, why you come
    to Australia?"

But the special film is my own
Memory of Mawalan.

Now there is a new way to operate coming up.
Before, we never look old person who passed away.
There is the new way to operate today,
before, even I myself not want to see face
my father's picture even on movie or photograph, but still I
    am changing because now I want to see
and show it to the family
because some of my young children, they don't know about
    my father,
even my own children, like Mayaṯili, Gomili, Mäpupu,
    Yalumul and Bayulma.
They haven't seen my father and that's why I want to get
    that film that *I* made.
I was been waiting for ten years from the Film Australia.

At last, I got it, I got it at home in Melbourne,
that is a sort of home for me, or really is for Jenny.

Before we don't want to see picture of a dead person or
    dead person.
If we saw those days we used to have been very
    unhappy, crying,
still it's coming now
to see what old people have been doing before.

NOTES

Wandjuk's orientation towards nature was always profoundly spiritual. During his visits to capital cities and regional centres as a member and then Chairman of the Aboriginal Arts Board, he was frequently asked to inspect Aboriginal art engravings, or archaeological sites. His sense of loss and sadness on these journeys was intense – he realised that the images and symbols were made by distant kin who no longer lived and he felt the vulnerability of his own song and culture. These visits intensified his need to teach the young people at Yirrkala about sacred things.

When we visited a special area, an engraving or painting, he would look around, observe the structure of the landscape, the formation of rocks, the relationship of plants, trees, unusual features, and so on, then interpret this from his own cultural perspective, from his "feeling". This interpretative role was not initially accepted by professional Balanda in the field, particularly some senior National Parks and Wildlife staff who had responsibility for the care of rock engravings. In the 1970s the philosophy was that if Aboriginal people who were the original owners of the area had not handed down the origin or meaning of these ancient marks, they could therefore not be interpreted by Aborigines from other areas. However, compared to a Balanda scientific orientation, Wandjuk's contribution was distinct and profound. He frequently interpreted the entire land formation in relation

to the art, engraving or painting, and opened himself to receive the story or song from any spirits who might still be, in his words, "waiting there because they knew I was a man of the law". The incidents he describes briefly here reveal his reaction.

The Colo River site in New South Wales is a large ancestral figure on Wheelbarrow Ridge Road. The song that he received in a dream later that day is still sung and known by the family. Receiving songs from spirit ancestors in a dreaming trance state is a perfectly authentic way for men of high degree to receive spiritual information. In addition the figure reminded Wandjuk of Wawilak. A road cuts between the rock engraving and other rocks he speaks of as "not a real painting but a sort of painting". These are in fact eroded, weathered sandstone ripples, a natural feature, not man-made, but to him an integral part of the entire spiritual place, a feature made by the ancestral figure engraved there.

It is obvious why his total interpretation involving sun, sea, earth, sky and spirit were dangerous to those entrusted with the care of rock engravings – it was simpler, and less costly, to regard only the simple markings on the rock as important to preserve, not the entire cliff or bluff. Our world does not perceive nature in that way.

On another visit to the New South Wales country he interpreted newly rediscovered whale engravings after a

bush fire swept through the sandstone hills behind the beach at Dee Why, northern Sydney. He believed this was a very large teaching area for ceremony relating to the whale. The very ridge the whale was carved on was shaped like the rounded back of a whale facing the sea. Historic records show that Aboriginal whale feasts did in fact take place when whales seasonally beached themselves on the sands beneath the bluff.[18]

Wandjuk's interpretative roles at southern Aboriginal art sites was appreciated far more by Aborigines than by Balanda. On his earliest visits to Sydney he would occasionally remark that southern Aborigines "knew nothing" but as he visited the sacred places, and learnt the stories of social and cultural destruction, family breakdown, massacres, distress and grief, he became sympathetic and aware of the vulnerability of his own world. He strove wherever possible to help Aborigines from all other areas in Australia in their programs of cultural revival, offering them songs, interpretations and time whenever he could.

---

[18] As this book goes to press, a young whale has beached itself at the same place. The news bulletins speak of scientific confusion about the reason for this – Mawalan II finds the answer in his father's explanation. This whole area is a sacred whale place, but as the religious custodians are no longer there to explain things to us, we remain ignorant.

POWER ON THIS EARTH

When I was working on the Aboriginal Arts Board, Jenny Isaacs and me meet each other, and then we meet one of the man, NPWS[19] ranger, and he take us to the sacred site, or sacred area, which is a drawing, a whale drawing, and then I knew, I knew what it is. There's a symbol belong to this area, belong to Sydney area that the Aboriginal people have lost – no one ever know what that design or drawing on the rock or cave, but I know.

This is the first time the Aboriginal tribal man like me travel into the city, because all the other archaeology people, Balanda, thought nobody know, they think every different Aboriginal people from other world is lost, gone, don't know much about it. They do. But some, because they brought up in Balanda way, they don't know.

But I'm the man who is coming to the city to visit
    different area
to see the paintings
and have a feeling, feeling sad.
It is sad feeling really
something there
power on this earth.

Wandjuk Marika travelled to special Aboriginal areas throughout Australia to protect sacred sites and to interpret their meaning.

One day, Guyana and Miwura[20] took me into bush some-
    where, maybe the Colo River 55 kilometres away.
I can see it still.
Anyway they took me there
and I thought "there's nothing"
but then there's the special tree and the mark or drawing –
    the Dreaming Creation was sitting there.
And there is the painting,
it's on the rock, not a real painting, but a sort of painting,
just like my own design,

---

19 National Parks and Wildlife Service.
20 David and Jennifer Isaacs.

At rock formations or engravings,
Wandjuk would interpret the meaning
of the whole area – "not just the mark".

and when I was put my foot on that area, I was sad
and I was crying
because there is a power, there is a symbol.
On the other hand, I was crying because nobody
    ever know
no one ever been there or able to care for that area,
care for that special area,
no one know.
They have lost,
and that's why I am trying to put this word in this book,
so they can know.
There's so many things,
so many paintings in the cave all over Australia.

And then I come back to Sydney I working in Aboriginal Arts Board, what, why, how we going to preserve all the sacred sites – are we going to fence them? I try to help to search the area so no one able to go to. That's what I was talking to the Arts Board when I was working but nothing happened. They said, "Yes, yes, but we need to be changing." Maybe this new Board they have now today, they do the same thing as I did – or maybe not, just talking or something else – instead of to find the place which is have been lost, the place where everything is forgotten.

Then I fly over to Newcastle, and Bill Smith meet me there, and took me into the mountain, and showed me the drawing in the cave, painting, similar paint like Laura Cave, Quinkan country, and then I said,
    "Yes, this is a spirit country" and then he took me
      other places,
    where a man was sneaking and there was a crocodile, a huge
      crocodile – changed into crocodile,
    that area used to be water or sea,
    and the man was sneaking and there's some people
      in Dreaming,
    and the crocodile was turning into rock.
    Real crocodile and the man was standing – you could see
      the face and the body,
    and I told him, "This is the special area."

    Now, when I was meet Bill Smith somewhere,
    I don't know where, maybe last year or maybe this year
    he told me that area have been fencing already, protecting
    because the Aboriginal people in Newcastle they working
      on it –
    every place I went to, they protecting
    and also there's a rock and a tree.
    The woman turn into a tree, the same area where's the
      crocodile on the hill.

When I was saw these things,
I did the same thing,
feel sad but feeling very strong
– there is the power there.

Some of these places I went to
I not feel like I want to go back home.
I like to stay there,
get to know more about the story, the knowledge
or find somebody in that area to tell me more about how
    that been happening there.

Then I went to western district, Victoria, the place called
    Lake Condah.
That region is the rock fish trap for Aboriginal people,
a certain time here they get the fish –
they build long fish trap,
and they used to live on the rock on the top of the hill.
When I walking there the Balanda said to me,
"This is the place where they make fish trap –
    Aboriginal people."
That what archaeologist said to me, Peter Coutts,
he thought that and told me all about it.
But in **my** eye and in **my** feeling it were different –
that's the snake story.
You can see the snake, all of it
and people who built the rock, there, on top of the hill,
to protect themselves from snake.

It doesn't matter if I'm from the north,
if I come down to that special place, I feel sad,
and then something come into my mind to think
and I concentrate very hard,
and then the old man or the Creation ancestor
come to me in the dream
and he say, "OK, this place is not different from your area,
this dreaming snake travel from south to top
and you can see the place here.
Our spirit is here, we lucky – now you go through again to
    show to the Balanda.
They don't know what in this place.
This is a special and sacred area."
That's what I was dreaming
I just heard the voice, belonging to that area.[21]

Engraving of Ancestor figure in the Hawkesbury River area of New South Wales. Wandjuk visited this place and many others with rangers and Aboriginal custodians to give his own interpretation.

---

21 Later, inspired by Lake Condah, Wandjuk painted a special design on bark and
    presented it to the Gunditj Mara people of Victoria, the land owners.

Wandjuk Marika at Yalaŋbara, source of his wisdom and knowledge about the land and spirit world.

After this fish trap we went to one of the caves
which is a special area,
not allow any women to go on that area –
that area is for initiation ceremony to put young man
    through to the Law,
the special area there.
And there's all the different painting there,
like the snake, like the goanna, like kangaroo,
emu, footprint, man, figure in that cave
and I was walking through that area
and stand on that ground
and then the spirit said to me on that hill,

"Look, Wandjuk, you're on the special area,
I know you are elder and I know you are the law.
Now we want you to stay right here,
so we can give you more story about what been happening
to our people here."

I did, I not want to go back.
I wanted to stay right there.
This is in western district, Victoria, and then Peter Coutts and Jenny Home say, "Come on let's go, let's go home" and I say, "No, I don't want to, I feel I'm going to stay right here by myself. Someone will looking after me, because the spirit on that area not bad spirit, but good spirit – the Creation spirit said to me, 'We want you to stay here, you are one of us.'" I hear the song. But now I forget.

I forget that song from Victoria, but I have the song from the first place, Colo River, I was crying and Jenny Isaacs was pats my back, and she said to me, "Don't cry, don't cry, we'll take care of you." And I said to Jenny Isaacs,
"Now this is the place, most important place,
the same design as the Wawilak story."
And then we went back home and I was sleepy.
The door was closed and I was falling asleep.
I could hear this voice outside.
Beard is longer than mine and he was singing outside
the house,
near the doorway and he is singing this one.
Wawilahnah is the Wawilak song.

Wawilahnah
Wawilahnah
Wuruŋalmi
Wuruŋalmi
Guwawuru
Dhumundurr

Wawilahnah is the Wawilak herself.
Dhumundurr is that hill or the rock where we stand.
Guwawuru or Wuruŋalmi is the scrub or bush, you can say
– "We were walking, on that area"
and then the spirit was said to me,
"Don't worry, don't be scared."
The door was closed but the cat came in.
I don't know how it came in and it was sitting,
he took my bed and I saw only half of the chest,
I saw only his face.
That's some of the story of what been happening in my life in Balanda's world.

MIYALK – WOMEN

NOTES

In his active social life in southern cities, Wandjuk always appreciated the friendship and company of women. Many in turn were attracted to his poetic ways, his spiritual nature and entrée to another world. To some this seemed at odds with his status as an important political leader and ceremonial head in Arnhem Land, and indeed I once asked him why he sought out women so often in Sydney and other places.

His answer was simple "But, Galay, you know the reason. I have told you many times so you can understand, I am a **man**, I am **the** man. I am the son, of the son, of the son from the father and the grandfather and the grandfather before that…from Djaŋkawu. Djaŋkawu create all the children. He create the tribes and I am **the man** descended from **him**."

This is just the story of the miyalk, the woman, I have two wives, and I have Jenny Home and she, we, have a little girl, the princess Mayatili.

I meet so many miyalk around the world. I travelling meet 100 Balanda miyalk but only cuddle or hug for make me not lonely. I'm travelling, always talking. I'm fed up travelling. In Russia I meet a miyalk. She was full naked, take off her clothes, and look me full naked show herself to me. That in the motel or hotel, whatever they call it in the Russia language. We can't talk each other. She talk in Russia language, I am speaking in English. Nothing, anything galay, I'm not going to muck around with the miyalk. (That shock me galay, shock to my eye.) Yolŋu miyalk never show to ḏirramu (man) like that, I'm not talking about just the top part.

Yes, anyway. There is another miyalk in New Zealand and she have one of my children. I meet her at the New Zealand Maori culture festival, Pacific Arts. I am the chairman, Aboriginal Arts Board and we go there for dance, talk. They have a ceremony. And there is the miyalk.

Miyalk everywhere, they like to know full blood Aboriginal man. Doesn't matter old or young women – long as they happy in the body. But then, in Sydney, I was go for have a drink, gurtha gapu, fire water (just a short time galay (wife), not getting drunk, yaka!) The märrma (two) miyalk cut my beard, steal the hairs, when I was asleep.
>   That make me furious
>   I was very very angry.
>   In that beard is the power, like my father Mawalan.
>   When I was a young boy I always look my father's.
>   Then I grow the beard, same like my father.
>   And those miyalk, maybe one miyalk, maybe two, they just laugh,
>   say, "Sorry Wandjuk.
>   I want to keep your hairs to remember."

148

But I say, "No!" And I nearly hit her.
If I hit her she will die.

Some miyalk they want rupiah – $20, $30 but then my wallet is gone! They are bad miyalk!
Then, maybe two days, or 2 months,
I am feeling weak, the miyalk have my hair – maŋi maŋi.
I was sitting, and sometimes I drinking gapu, little bit
fire gapu
and feeling happy.
But then I was not concentrate.
Maybe the pay-back is going to happen.

Yoku Yoku my little brother say to me,
"Come here big brother, wäwa,
maybe the Balanda medicine can help you become strong."
Then he make the Balanda "marrŋgitj'" (sorcerer) medicine
on my mind.
It's like the Yolŋu, we do like that but ours is a more power-
ful.
He give me something strong, put on my head, and I can
feel strong like a spear.
I can fight the maŋi maŋi, have more power.

After that I stay home. Then I meet Jenny Home. She is the **strong** woman, always help me but yaka, I'm not talking or looking other miyalk (she like you, galay, strong woman, yaka fire gapu).

NOTES

When a Yolŋu person dies, the spirit travels quickly to those closest, appearing to them in a dream or by message from a bird. This happened frequently to Wandjuk when he was visiting the south. He would wake, disturbed and worried something was wrong, with an accurate premonition of just who it was that had died. This phenomenon though not exclusive to Yolŋu is common to many Aboriginal people throughout Australia.

One of the central conflicts in Wandjuk's dual lives in both Balanda and Yolŋu worlds was his repeated abrupt exits from Balanda meetings to return home when he was required for a funeral. His input at funerals was essential. He would often sit quietly after such a dream visitation, ring home, issue instructions, then calculate how many days leeway he had before arrangements in the north were ready. At these times intense pressure was often exerted from both sides – from Balanda for him to remain at the "negotiating table" due to plane and meeting costs, protocol, and the need for Aboriginal input, and from the Yolŋu family for similar reasons but with the added and uncompromisingly decisive reason that he was needed to ensure that the spirit of the deceased would be properly treated in order to return to it's "spirit home".

Yolŋu funerals are not one-day events as in the Balanda world. They may last months and involve the travel of several hundred kin from far places to the funeral ground (depending on the status of the deceased). They require extensive planning, financing and organisation of hospitality. The songs and dances are performed episodically each day close to the immediate bereaved family who are camped in isolation with the body. Great funeral ceremonies are the climax of life and explore all the Yolŋu arts – body and coffin painting, feather and string regalia, making of sacred emblems, song cycles and powerful emotive dancing. Wandjuk was needed to fulfil his managerial role as the "mortuary man".

FUNERALS

I was sleeping in Sydney and I was screaming and talking in the night crying, and in the morning I went to the office, but I was still on dreaming, but I went to the office (Arts Board office) crying and talking in the morning and I tell all the story about that dreaming and they say, "No."

> Then I ring to home.
> "Yes, you have to come, it's true."
> Nobody ever told me, I was just asking.
> Then they said my brother passed away,
> "How come you know?" they said.
> "I know because my feeling in my body is a different one.
> I can see what is going on in my body."

Anyhow they book me a special flight and they ring up the airline, I was on the plane, crying always, all day. I see the sign, the painting, in my mind.[22] When I go back I have to show them because Mawalan II he know a special song, he know some of the painting, even better than me. Real djanda (goanna), I'm just painting Yolŋu way back but he can draw the djanda just like painting in the modern paints, water paint, because he's doing watercolour and painting like I used to do, with a pencil or watercolour. He's just learning, but I say to him, "No, we have to do properly", and he did. He did painting Yalaŋbara; track of Djaŋkawu from water up.

> A funeral is most important to our people,
> to me especially because they want me, need me to be there
> to organising my ceremony for this ghost.
> I have to organise what the ceremony we're going to singing

---

22 Wandjuk had a vision, or a revelation of a sacred design – which he knew came from his brother's spirit – a new arrangement of designs for the sunrise at Yalaŋbara. He later painted it.

Opposite: *Three of Wandjuk's sons stand in dignified attendance during the funeral of Roy Daḏayŋa Marika, Chairman of the Dhanbul Council. From left: Wuyula, Djaybiny, Mawalan.*

151

The women gather to perform the dance of the Wawilak sisters. The sisters and the children are around the sacred djuta. When they plunge their digging sticks into the ground, a freshwater hole is formed. Dancers include: Milirrpum (far left), Wukaka (kneeling), Dadayŋa (with clap sticks), Laŋani, Wandjuk's sister (in white dress) and Wandjuk (far right).

today, or tomorrow or next day.
Are we going to sing on [about] the land or seaside
or on the beach or in the spirit land.
How the spirit people have been come together and made
    individual things,
like feathers,
or collect from special flower, darraŋgulk, which is
    the flower
so they can make a morning star out of that feathers,
or they might get the bird feather like white cockatoo, land
    seagull or ibis,
Yes like ibis, barrir-barrir (rainbow bird) and ṉurruṉurru
    which is spoonbill,
or brolga, ḏaŋgultji.
All these birds they are collecting, the spirit people,
    Dhanbul people,
to make the feathers for the morning star.

That's what they want me to go through,
doesn't matter there or here,
I am the man,
doesn't matter whoever passed away in Yirrkala,
what his tribe, what his language, where he from,
or from which homeland –
they looking at me for funeral.

Because all their fathers and father's fathers they come to Yirrkala in the first place, bring all their wives, they make children there, and all their children is grew up with the woman or the man to settle down Yirrkala because they can't establish their own homeland. They looking at me very close because I am the owner of the land and all the people, the community, have belong to Yirrkala, they brought up in Yirrkala, they born in Yirrkala, when they grew up become man and woman they moving up to get married. There's the people they gets more and more and more, in the main place, which is Yirrkala, my land, and they are my children and the children for my land.

That's why they looking at me and they want me to deal with the funerals. I'm not going to be miss any ceremony, doesn't matter whoever passed away, Yirritja or Dhuwa, different group of people, but they still need me, they think of their fathers my grandfathers who had been come to establish and settle down in Yirrkala to raise the people today.

It is far across the land, to the spirit home.
Still they need me to go and involve on that ceremony,
because I am the land owner,
and they're children of Yirrkala.

Wedu performing the sacred power dance of the Djaŋkawu during Mawalan's funeral memorial.

Not only that, but I know more, more experience about the ceremony and about the song, the ordinary song or public song and important dancing and important ceremony or song. Also, their fathers have been passed away so quick, they didn't have any time to teach them, their own children, but now this is my time, I can do something, so they can be holding and carrying on with their children's children to come.

The Christian church, prayer, put it into ground, throw the earth or sand on top of the coffin, that ridiculous, and that's the Balanda way of looking at it, so the spirit go to Heaven.

But now ***this is*** the difference for Yolŋu.

In **my** way
I was dancing
I was singing with the body
yes we put the body or coffin into the ground,
but the singing is what's happening.

It is most important because we felt sorry for her or him,
that she not staying and not with us
because we have sadness, we have sorry,
so we sing, make ourselves happy
and farewell that man or woman singing that we not going
    to see her or him any more
and sing we will meet each other in the spirit land,
and we make preparations to make that body happy
to remind us when he or her go into the spirit land.

So their spirit will be in good hands to go through to the new spirit land. I am the man responsible for **inside** Djaŋkawu song or ceremony. That's why they wait for me. Even Yirritja, whether Dhalwaŋu or Gumatj, I'm still responsible for Barama and Laintjuŋ because I've been go through it.

My own father passed away in 1967, I didn't say the name of my father (me and my family we use other name, which is exactly the same pronunciation or spelling like my young brother). In 1978 then we changed the name and now we call my father's name. About 10 years and I will change the name and call my father's name.

Today we call Mawalan.

We don't want to hear too early the name of the
    dead person.
If we calling too early
maybe month or week or year,
then we feel sad and everybody screaming and yelling
    and crying
because too early for the people who have passed away,
to call their names
and also when they call the name – the spirit turn back.

The spirit hear it, hear the name and turn back to the family
and they hang around there
or maybe the spirit might hurt them or kill and bring them
    to them.

You can't send the spirit away, unless we can have a
    big ceremony.
Big ceremony like we call Waṉtjurr or Bukulup.

Waṉtjurr is like big branches of a tree
we make special ground, put the wood and everybody
    sit around,
make the fire and singing and put those leaves,
make it warm, whip ourselves,
get rid of the spirit, make ourselves free –
or we can make the same hole, dig a hole, get the water,
    pour it over
and wash all of our face.
That's what you call the cleansing ceremony.
Yes, cleansing, that's what we call bukulup,
the cleaning of ourselves with water,
and Waṉtjurr we call Djaladada [branches],
Waṉtjurr is hole in special ground we put hole and make
    steam with branches.
One is water and one is fire.

The wife or the mother of that dead man,
we have to paint a special design on her body, to make
    her free
wash the dead man's sweat because the dead man and she
    they sleep together,
and we whip her with the branches
everyone, not only one, everyone turns around her in a circle.
The girl is very unhappy and very sad
because she lose her beloved husband, that she loved him.
All the wives.
The children, they're painting too.
When if I'm going to passed away I don't know who going
    to be around these ceremony,
maybe my son or whoever they learning right now.

There's got to be a ceremony with this – that's why I'm teaching my
own children and my own tribe, Rirratjiŋu tribe, clan. Wukaka's sons
and daughter and Roy's sons and daughter.

The old man passed away and last month, my auntie passed away,
same thing. Now we have a big ceremony coming up, they still waiting for me, for the rain, or for blankets, trousers, books, also shoes,
dress. We make one coffin to put all in, one for my auntie and another coffin for old man, not old man, young, after me, you know.
Everything is already there, but they're waiting for me. When we
ready we going to take to Yalaŋbara and make a big ceremony there.

*Wandjuk and the family prepare to take
part in the funeral of their waku – son
(Rirratjiŋu people are 'mother' clan to
Gumatj). Rärriwuy paints Mayakaŋu in
foreground, behind are Gotjiriŋu and
Wayalwaŋa mixing the clay paint.*

We bury the clothes. Used to be burning, but now has changed. Other things too. Yes, we going to bury them with the coffin, with the body, and, at the same time, I'm going to make a Djaŋkawu manikay (song ritual).

Before I go more further I just remember about my children that I have lost. From first wife I have lost two, one girl and one little boy, from the second wife I lost one girl. I hope I am not going to lose again.

Yes, when I lost those children (from first and second wives) I had a big ceremony – two together. I lose them before their grandfather had been passed away. On those years I was been sad, singing all along, make the ceremony and make the very special sacred object or implement or dilly bag or feathers to remind me and think of the children I have lost – and remind me where they belong.

The little girl was maybe one years old, and the big boy is about four years old, and the other little girl was two years old from the second wife. And then all along I make the special dilly bag, special feathers – they belong and are Djaŋkawu children, we are the Djaŋkawu children, we call ourself Mayarr Mayarr.

> The Djaŋkawu children or Mayarr Mayarr have two names.
> Not only the Rirratjiŋu but also Boyuyukululmi.
> We are most important tribe, Mayarr Mayarr.
> They singing the songs Djaŋkawu, Wawilak and Dhanbul.
> Dhanbul is Mururruma song.

Now, we go back, not long ago I have lost my brother, my dear brother, baby brother. I made a special sacred object to thank him because he was been learning like me. He should have been take over after me but they have been jealous of him and do something about it, something Yolŋu culture because those days had been a big jealousy because my father and me and my young brother been more important people at knowledge and ways, that's why they destroyed my brother's life. After that I made a special Djaŋkawu object to give him and bury with the body.

> Now I still have that other one,
> which is remembrance of my father,
> we still got that there,
> it has the name after my father, Mawalan.
> I tried to get rid of that and bury it with my brother's body,
> because he is dear to my heart, my brother,
> but Mawalan II said to me, "No, daddy, I need that,
> so I can learn through that sacred object,

'cause you're getting old, never know what will be
    happening to you",
and I said to him, "OK" and we still got it.

Everything in Yolŋu, in my life and my family's life, not only my own
people or tribe or clan, individual tribe have the similar the same,
whatever they do, whoever they lose, they do exactly the same as I do.

After my father's time, if any other tribe have been passed away they
always come and ask for us for help to sent or give our own sacred
string, sacred feathers to help them, no matter whoever they are, but
today is still the same, we do the same thing because they need our
help. We are kind, respectable and top people, very knowledgeable.

I don't know if I finish this life story. They want me to come finish
that manikay buŋgul for the funeral. I don't know, look like I'm the
yindi buŋgul for funeral – mortuary. Yes. I'm the mortuary man. I'll
have to go book plane straight to Gove and then go MAF[23] book
straight to Biranybirany.

*The burial ground of great Rirratjiŋu men.
The grave of Wandjuk's father Mawalan
is on the left, decorated at the close of the
memorial ceremony, some years after
his death.*

---

23 Missionary Aviation Fellowship

TEACHING MY CHILDREN

NOTES

Since this chapter was recorded by Wandjuk in 1985–86, sadly some of his children are no longer living. Their names have been changed in the book in keeping with the wishes of the family.

In the intervening years since Wandjuk's death, his children have grown up; even his youngest son, Gomili, is now married. Some have changed jobs, new grandchildren have been born. Mawalan II has now completed a radio announcer course at Batchelor College; Rärriwuy is a senior teacher at the school and takes responsibility for many of the younger family members. Mayaṯili is now a secondary school student. She travels regularly to Yirrkala and participates in ceremonies there.

Opposite: *Playing in the white sands of Yalaŋbara. From left: Djopani, Birralimi, Yuwatjpi, Bakatjarri – grandsons of Wandjuk Marika.*

I found out about promised wife when I was about eight
    years of age
then I was not feel like I going to married.
I just walk round
because I want to learn and clear my mind,
but her parents are been telling me,
"Come on Wandjuk, come and marry our daughter, because
    our time is run out.
If we going to live separately like you, still single,
then what you going to do and what she going to do.
Are you going to lose her or do you still want to marry her?"
Then I still couldn't say anything,
but my parents were saying to her parents,
and so I took her and looking after her
and then my parents were saying I'll have to say yes, I'll
    have to marry her.
She was about 16, because I want to make myself clear in
    my mind.

After marriage, problems and fighting, 'cause sometimes she is happy and sometimes she is unhappy. And then I married this other one, only about 15 years of age, so I been looking after two wives till I was about 16 years of age. I can't understand it, big problem, fighting with second wife, she always playing with some other people, running away, sneaking away to another tribe, or another relative and I was fighting like mad. Usually most young wives do that. But then I take her away from the family to stay by herself, between me and my wife, no one is around her, right in the bush or we on the island, so we can stay and be happy and talk so that she can understand who I am, that I love her and she love me, that I am her promised husband. I take them my two wives in the bush, I come down and talk to them and show them around the country. Still I have a problem with the young one in the bush. She always running away, go with the other people, I still used to chasing her and bringing her back, and then I take her to the island so she settle down.

Wuyula, Mawalan, Gomili and their father Wandjuk Marika in Sydney before leaving for Canada, 1986.

I was get married about 1950,
get married the first wife.
Her name is Gotjiriŋu and Wurrapa is a clan name.
I have from her, four girls and one boy.
The first one from the first wife is my daughter,
    Warraŋgilŋa,
the second one is Helen [mother of Maxine], and the third
    one is Rärriwuy,
the fourth one is Wayalwaŋa,
and the boy is Wuyula,
and also I lose two child from the first one,
a boy, a little boy, and a little girl.
The little girl's name is Gubilyun, deceased,
and the boy's name is Birripi.
Those one girl and one boy I lose from the first wife.

And then my second wife is the sister of the eldest wife. First I marry eldest and then I marry the younger sister of the first one (from the same mother and father).

The second wife is Dhuwandjika and now, from her,
    second one,
I have five boys, Mawalan is the first one after the first girl.
After Mawalan the first boy, is Bakili a girl,
those two are married now, brother and sister married,
and then Marrirriwuy the third one
and Napandala the fourth one
and two boys Yalarrma and Gomili, the two boys.
Now I repeat them, five boys, Mawalan, Marrirriwuy or
    Djaybiny, Mäpupu, Gomili.
Yes. I have the six children from the second wife.

Then I adopted a little girl,
from Djapu clan into Rirratjiŋu
into my family, as my daughter.
Her name is Lucille Dhawunyilnyil.
Dhawunyilnyil means fish trap,
the circles of rock we made to catch the fish.

The children two from the first one, they all married,
one eldest of her daughter is a married woman now,
and then she had four, five boys and two girls,
and my second daughter
Helen only have one girl, Maxine.
My third daughter have three boys
and the fourth one have three boys and two girls.
Three boys and two girls, that's what I'm going to tell you.

OK from the second wife my son Mawalan have one child,
   one daughter,
which is Gayana,
and my daughter have four boys and one girl
and the second daughter have only one girl,
but all the boys Marrirriwuy, Gomili, Yalarrma, Mawalan,
   Wuyula, they all single.
All my daughters married, and one, my son, married,
but the other boys haven't married, they still single.
They have a promise,
but I don't know when they going to married,
they promise one, but I don't know.

Yes. Then I was been travelling around in the bush
go around teach them culture, teach them about the laws,
and then they went to school.
My daughter, Helen, she is a teaching assistant in homeland
   centre, Gurrumuru, Arnhem Bay,
and the third one, Rärriwuy,
already have a teaching job, or flying teaching or visiting
   teaching education,
and then the fourth one, Wayalwaŋa,
she's working on the store, a shop staff.
Mawalan is name is after my father's name,
second name, number two name Dhuwirriya, third
   name Djawulu,
and he's working on bilingual program or bilingual
   education,
drawing and writing about Yolŋu and Balanda's work.
And then all the other children are still on school,
but Marrirriwuy is out and he start to work learning about
   building or engineering.

I want them to be know and learn more about the work and the land and culture. Now from the second wife, Mawalan have learn more about their own culture, about the painting and the singing. Marrirriwuy is start to learning, all the boys, like Marrirriwuy (Djaybiny), or Wuyula (Mukuwatbuy), Yalarrma (Mäpupu) or Barrada is start. And Gomili, they all learn about the Yolŋu culture and at the same time they learn about the Balanda way. I'm happy these three girls, they have a good job, teaching at school and also Mawalan have job on bilingual programs. and all the others are just learning.

I need them to be take my djuta (walking stick from the special tree), follow my step, when I'm been passed away so they can carry on with their life, their future life, like they start learning now about the culture, so they can have both side like I did. Like I have Balanda and Yolŋu. First they want to learn about the Yolŋu culture, while I am

Acrylic painting on artists' board by Wandjuk's son Mawalan, 1990. Yalaŋbara.

Mawalan is now the primary custodian of Yalaŋbara.

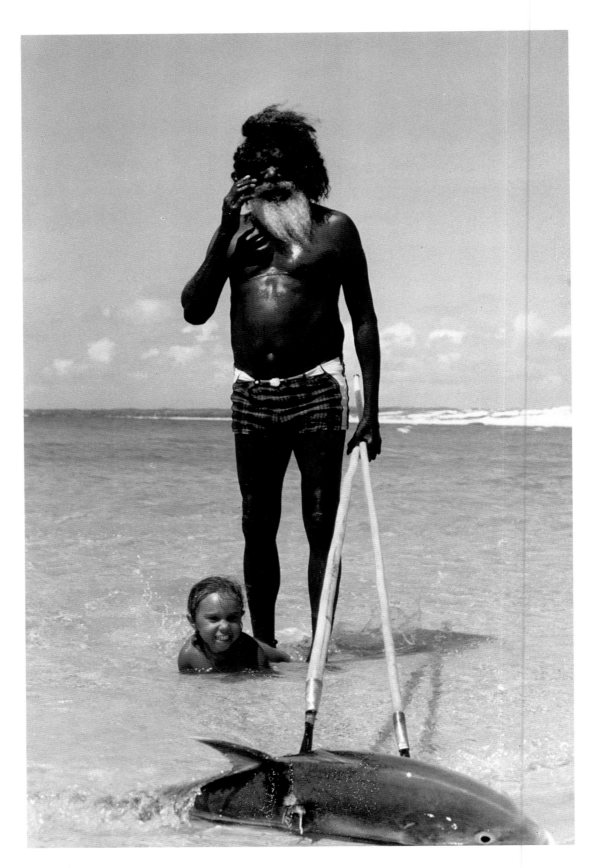

Above: *Descendants and family of Wandjuk Marika at the funeral of Roy Daḏanga Marika, MBE. From top left: Mawalan, Mäpuṗu, Giyakmin, Djaybiny, Napandala (obscured), Mayaṯili, Läṇani, Wayalwaṇa, Wuyula, Dhuwarrwarr, Rärriwuy, Maxine's mother, Bakitju, Djayminy, Marrnyurama, Warrṇgilṇa, Buṇumbirr, Miwura, Rorr'wuy and Balpaḏaṇan (Wandjuk's dog).*

Left: *Rärriwuy Marika.*

Opposite: *Wandjuk Marika and Mayaṯili with a large nuykal (trevally), to be shared with the family camped at Yalaṇbara.*

163

Birralimi, Wandjuk and Gomili at breakfast time at Yalaṇbara.

alive, like their grandfather was teaching me, the older culture, the older law, older ceremony. I want them to be like that. I am always talking to them.

When my children was passed away, two girls and one boy that's the most sad and bad day for me. Hardly ever control myself with the crying, thinking about the child, very sad. I used to walk thinking about something else. When I lost the three children, two girls, one boy. One girls and one boys from the first wife and one girls from the second wife, Burrilimawuy and that was a sad time, very unhappy days. We used to hate some other people, complain about other people maybe they do bad thing to our children or maybe they damage the body or mind, that the sort of thing we complaining about. From the first wife the children fight each other. Maybe they damage their brain or leg or back or head, they always say to us, the doctor was telling me, "You got bad children, your sons – somebody has been damaging their body or rib." My daughter from the second wife, she was get drowned right on the river, Yirrkala Creek, maybe somebody get and pushed her down or sink her down and put their foot. Very sad days and unhappy days for us.

Like when I have been sad for two years for my father that I have lost, 1967, 1968, 1969 I start to travel and then I meet you. It's a long time. And that then I been go back to home and then do a little bit of work and I start to get the Aboriginal Arts Board job, Chairman. First I was member, 1973 to 1976, then I become Chairman of the Aboriginal Arts Board Council and then I went back – I still do my work, and then I found my third wife.

And then I have a third wife, which is Baĺanda, and her name is Jenny Home. Yolŋu name I give her is Wulula and I have a little girl with her, Mayaṯili, the Balanda name I give her, Mary Jane, but we don't often call her the Balanda name, we always call her the Yolŋu name, Mayaṯili. Now it is only the singular, not the plural. Miss Mayaṯili Marika. It is only three years old, now this year will be four years old.

1977 we known each other, four years later in 1980 we come together and went to Yirrkala, 1980. We were there established a place in Yalaṇbara for the family, all the family move up there. We were staying at Yalaṇbara for quite a long time and she goes back and forth, and then she get big job teaching last year in the school in the postprimary, and the little girl she always go to preschool. Now she is talking three languages, Balanda language, her father's language and relation language.

In future Mayaṯili will be still able to help her family if they have a problem

have to bring these three girls together so that I can talk to them, so they can know and learn about what my work is.

> This is the book I'm written for them
> so they can be able to read
> and see and think.

But boys is OK. They have no problem. Mawalan is married already and he has a daughter and he is working on bilingual programs, and also he learn more about the song and the dancing and how to make special things, sacred object, and Marrirriwuy is to working as a carpenter. Sometimes he's working as a plumber or gardener and also Wuyula he's working, sometimes he is in school, but I been worried for two little boys, Mäpupu (Yalarrma), also Gomili. Gomili is a very quiet boy and he always go to the school, sometimes he go to school and sometime he just play around in natural way, bush learning how to hunt, how to make the spear, which is good, instead of just go to school, sitting there learn about something else, and the little boy, Yalumul, which is my brother's son (but I'm looking after him), sometimes he go to school, sometimes he just play around with the children but I leave them to be work together, go to school, learn more about it, like I used to do.

I like to do both, in my own life, learn about my own world, how to hunt, learn about how to paint, or go through the bush and hunting for a fish. At the same time I used to go to school and learn about more English way to read and write, and that why I have two culture.

> I want my children to carry on their own and do as I do
> in past.
> I want my children to work, learn two culture.
> Yolŋu culture and Balanda culture
> in two worlds,
> our own world and Balanda's world,
> because the Yolŋu have our own world.

> We know what in it,
> in the earth,
> trees' names, birds' name, grass name, rivers' name and
> animals' name,
> not only on the land, but also on the sea.
> Doesn't matter what kind of sea creature, but we know
> the name of the sea creature,
> same as we know the land creature.

Early morning at Yalaŋbara, photographed by Wandjuk's grandson Bakatjarri Yunupiŋu. From left: Wandjuk, his first wife Gotjiriŋu, Miwura (Jenny Isaacs), his second wife Dhuwandjika and daughter Giyakmin.

Notes

Wandjuk Djuwakan Marika died in Darwin hospital in June 1987. He had fallen ill a few days previously in Gove. The source of the illness could not be determined but he slipped quickly into a coma and was transferred to Darwin. The doctors diagnosed septicaemia although no external wound was visible upon examination. The family refused a post mortem. Wandjuk was flown back to Gove and, in keeping with the respect he attracted and his ritual status, his funeral extended over months. He is remembered by all Dhuwa of eastern Arnhem Land but particularly the sunrise Rirratjiŋu and all Mayarr Mayarr.

After extended mourning and long vigil near his grave, his first wife Gotjiriŋu died in 1988. His second wife Dhuwandjika, although weakened by emphysema, continued to watch over the children and grandchildren but died in 1990. Two daughters have also died within the last two years as victims of the appalling health conditions at Yirrkala. Balanda, indeed, as Wandjuk says "bring bad thing" and Yolŋu continue to suffer. His children headed ceremonially by Mawalan II carry on the work of maintaining law and culture in his name, and handing on the heritage he fought to uphold, to future generations of Mayarr Mayarr, children of Djaŋkawu.

GOODBYE

I need this book to show to the world
and to my children.
Sometimes I think back when I was a little boy
and I feel sad, just like I'm still teenage
or very young.
I am walking through the bush with my parents.

But this is what I am doing now.
I'm doing something for the world,
something for the children, our children's children.
One day they might be able to see each other
and work together, hand by hand, side by side.
Share the knowledge, experience happiness.

Yes, now my time is short,
I wish to you all best wishes and happiness always,
wherever you are, in different part of Australia
and to my own people, to my children,
especially, the children.
One day the children will be working on this.

Now time is short.
I think that is the end of my words,
I wish you all best wish
and happy and long life for you for ever.
Thank you and goodbye.

GLOSSARY

Balanda	white, European
barrir-barrir	kind of bird, rainbow bird
biwudalmi	flowers of waterlily
Bukulup	cleansing ceremony
bulayi	tin, metal, precious treasure
buma	kill, hit, beat
buŋgul	dance, ceremony, "business", rite, ritual
buwata	plains turkey
dharraŋgulk	tree with red flowers; bark is spun into bush string
daŋultji	brolga
dhanbul	morning star
dhaŋgi	tree and its edible fruit, white flowers, bark used as fish poison
djaladada	branches
dhatam	leaves
dhum thum	kangaroo, wallaby
dhuŋ	to stand up for my rights
dhuŋu	roots
didjeridu	drone pipe, yidaki
dirramu	man, male, boy, husband
djanda	goanna, lizard
Djaŋkawu	Creation ancestor and his two sisters
djorra	letter, book
djurrpun	evening star
djuta	walking stick made from a special tree, cf mawalan
doi	money
galay	wife, in kinship terms
galpawiri	squid's back
galpu	woomerah
gapu	water, fluid, liquid, beverage
gara	fish spear
gayit	shovel nose spear
gulwirri	palm with fan-type leaves and seeds like marbles
Gunapipi	sacred ceremony
gurrumattji	magpie goose

172

gurtha	fire
guyarra	stone-headed spear
lindirritj	rainbow lorikeet
lippa-lippa	canoe
luŋiny	long pipe
maḏayin	sacred, secret, holy, taboo; any sacred object; an important sacred ceremony
manaŋi	steal
mända	octopus
maŋgi maŋgi	poison dart
maŋirrigirri	black flying fox
manikay	song, music, ceremonial singing
manymak	good, fine, delicious, healthy
manymak	and then; well (in narrative)
märi	maternal grandmother , paternal grandfather
märrma	two
marrŋgitj	sorcerer (for healing not evil), doctor, Aboriginal healer, medicine man
mawalan	sacred walking stick of Djaŋkawu
Mayarr Mayarr	Djaŋkawu children
mayaya	frill-neck lizard
maypal	shellfish, crustacean
milirrk	hailstone
miyalk	woman, girl, wife, female
mulmu	grass, weed
munḏaka	tree which contains water
ŋänḏi	mother
ŋänitji	beverage, grog, strong drink
ŋapipi	uncle
ŋarali	tobacco, cigarette, a smoke
ŋatha	food
nulla nulla	club
ṉurruṉurru	spoonbill
räkay	water-reed
raŋga	sacred totem, ceremonial object
waku	son
walmurrmurr	plains turkey
Waṉtjurr	cleansing ceremony
waŋarr	totemic ancestors, culture heroes, sacred things
wapitja	walking or digging sticks
wäwa	brother, elder
wulma	thunderclouds
Wuyal	Dreamtime spirit person
yaka	no, not
yätj	bad, evil, ill
yiḏaki	didjeridu, drone pipe
yindi	big, large
Yolŋu	person, human, Aboriginal, black
yothu	child, baby, young animal, small

ACKNOWLEDGEMENTS

Jennifer Isaacs is most grateful to all who assisted in making this book, in particular:

- typing of manuscript: Carmel Pepperell, Meredith Aveling and Cressida Hall (notes)
- manuscript checking: Mawalan Marika, Rärriwuy Marika, Jimmy Barmula Yunupiŋu, Wayalwaŋa Marika and Mamburra Marika
- Yolŋu spelling: Rärriwuy Marika.

Many have generously offered historical photographs, particularly Margaret Tuckson, Ian Dunlop and Michael Friedel. Jenny Home provided treasured pictures from family moments of importance, and help with the manuscript over the years.

Others who gave moral support, accommodation or otherwise enable her to effect the publication of Wandjuk's *Life Story* and keep her promise to him include principally her own family David, Joe, Sam and Will Isaacs, as well as Margaret Connolly, Laurie Muller, Carol Dettmann, John Witzig, Rodney Hall and Neilma Gantner.

PHOTO CREDITS

Courtesy of the Aboriginal Arts Board, Australia Council, pp. 108, 143, 144 top & bottom.

Art Gallery of New South Wales: p. 36.

Courtesy of the Australia Council: p. 107 bottom right.

Courtesy of the Berndt Museum of Anthropology, University of Western Australia: p. 56 (C.H. Berndt), 15 & 104 (R.M. Berndt), 107 top.

Ross Bray: pp. 33, 65 bottom, 67, 126.

Courtesy of Ian Dunlop (Film Australia): cover (Philip Robertson), pp. 8 bottom, 38, 45, 138, 152, 153, 157.

Michael Friedel: pp. 9 top, 23, 25 top & bottom, 89, 95 bottom left, 99, 102 bottom, 107 bottom left, 139.

Juno Gemes: p. 102 top.

Jenny Home: pp. 9 bottom, 93, 96 bottom, 137, 155, 160, 162, 163 top, 166 top.

David Isaacs: pp. 28, 63, 68 top & bottom, 165.

Jennifer Isaacs: pp. 2, 7, 8 top, 10, 12, 18, 19, 20, 21, 22, 24, 29, 32, 34, 35, 40, 41, 42, 43, 44, 47, 54, 59, 60 top & bottom, 61, 92, 94 left & right, 95 top & bottom right, 96 top, 97, 127 top & bottom, 128, 146, 150, 159, 161, 163 bottom, 164, 166 bottom left & right, 167 top & bottom, 168, 170.

Courtesy of the Kelton Foundation: pp. 16, 76.

Robert McFarlane: pp. 122, 123 top & bottom, 124, 125.

Reg Morrison, pp. 80, 145.

Jan Reid: p. 39.

Jon Rhodes: p. 98.

Courtesy of the Speaker of the House of Representatives, Parliament House, Canberra: pp. 103, 105, 106.

Jennifer Steele: pp. 1, 26 left & right, 37, 69, 78, 79, 111, 115, 116, 120 left & right, 176.

Margaret Tuckson: pp. 14, 31, 50, 51, 52 top & bottom, 53 top & bottom, 55, 57, 65 top, 66 top & bottom, 70, 71, 77 top & bottom, 78, 85, 112 top & bottom, 113 top & bottom, 114, 117 top & bottom, 118, 119.

Bakatjarri Yunupiŋu: p. 169.

Map, p. 6: Cartodraft.

LIST OF PAINTINGS

p. 1 – Wandjuk Marika,1982. *Mawalan – the sacred walking stick of the Creation Ancestors.*

p. 16 – Wandjuk Marika, c. 1967. *Djanda (goannas) on the Djaŋkawu sand dunes.*

p. 21 – Mawalan Marika. *Detail of Yalaŋbara sunrise.*

p. 26 – Wandjuk Marika, 1982 *Sunrise with scrub turkey and goanna. Sunset with goannas returning home.*

p. 33 – Wandjuk Marika, c. 1972. *Djaŋkawu with his mawalan.*

p. 35 – Wandjuk Marika, 1979. *Milngurr: the sacred place of fresh water.*

p. 36 – Wandjuk Marika and Mawalan Marika, 1957. *Djaŋkawu giving birth to the people at Yalaŋbara.*

p. 37 – Wandjuk Marika, 1982. *The birth of the children of Yalaŋbara.*

p. 69 – Wandjuk Marika, 1982. *Daymirri, the sea creature.*

p. 76 – Mawalan Marika, 1957. *The reef of Ŋulwaḏuk with its sea animals.*

p. 78 – Wandjuk Marika, 1972. *Djaŋkawu and his two mawalan.*

p. 105 – Jackie Duṉḏiwuy Waṉambi, 1968. *Wuyal, one of the ancestors.*

p. 111 – Wandjuk Marika, 1982. *The dwelling place of the goannas.*

p. 115 – Wandjuk Marika, 1982. *Mururrama: songmaker ancestor.*

p. 116 – Wandjuk Marika, 1982. *Goannas and bustards.*

p. 120 – Wandjuk Marika, 1982. *The Wawilak sisters.*

p. 161– Mawalan Marika, 1990. *Yalaŋbara.*

p. 176 – Wandjuk Marika, 1982. *Resting place of the Djaŋkawu.*

INDEX

Bark painting by Wandjuk Marika, 1982.

Resting Place of the Djaŋkawu.

"When the Djaŋkawu first arrived at Yalaŋbara they saw the tracks and they wonder what this track, you can see the little marks here, the goanna tracks, the djanda tracks, and their brother asked the two sisters – because in way back generation time, the two sisters were the boss and the main creation sisters. The Djaŋkawu brother he always asked them what 'that' what 'this' is. They answer: 'This track is to lead us to the special place, to the very special sacred ground.' Then they walked up the sandhill to where they were going to settle. Six different tribes have been made there. See the six rectangle marks there. That's the different tribe, relative, clan at Bilapinya."

— Wandjuk Marika, 1984.